THE SACRIFICIAL RITUAL IN THE ŚATAPATHA BRĀHMAṆA

THE SACRIFICIAL RITUAL IN THE ŚATAPATHA BRĀHMAṆA

NAAMA DRURY

MOTILAL BANARSIDASS
Delhi :: Varanasi :: Patna

Indological Publishers & Booksellers
Head Office : 41-U.A., Bungalow Road, Delhi-110 007
Branches : 1. Chowk, Varanasi-1 (U.P.)
2. Ashok Rajpath, Patna-4 (BIHAR)

First Edition : Delhi, 1981

Printed in India
By Shantilal Jain, at Shri Jainendra Press,
A-45, Phase I, Industrial Area, Naraina, New Delhi-110 028
Published by Narendra Prakash Jain, for Motilal Banarsidass,
Bungalow Road, Jawahar Nagar, Delhi-110 007.

PREFACE

The choice of the material selected by me has been governed by four objectives. My first objective was to consider the material of the Śatapatha Brāhmaṇa in a comparative relationship to the major, illustrative material collected by Western scholars from cultures other than Brahmanic Indian. Western scholars have developed theories relative to sacrifice, usually from material derived from Primitive, Biblical, Classical, or Archaeological sources and only rarely with any reference to the Indian tradition, although the Yajurveda and the Śatapatha Brāhmaṇa (as ritual treatises for priests concerned with the sacrifice) have been available in translation since the turn of the century.

Brahmanic material does not disprove theories presented by the scholars, and in some cases appears to contain classic examples of such theories. Nevertheless, the Brahmanic material does augment our knowledge of sacrifice and introduces us to unexpected theological nuances by emphasising aspects of sacrifice not previously considered important, or not considered at all. The completed fire altar represented a golden man seated in a golden bird, pointed towards the sun. In this, as in other rituals, Brahmanic sacrifice passes beyond any possible comparison with the known sacrifices of other cultures.

My second objective was to reduce portions of the voluminous Śatapatha Brāhmaṇa to basic patterns of ritual. It is my belief that the importance of this classic of rituals to Indian and comparative studies, and the intrinsic interest of its content, have been overlooked because it is obscured by the Brahmanic style. After a lifetime devoted to the translation of the Śatapatha Brāhmaṇa into English, Julius Eggeling wrote of it as "of wearisome prolixity of exposition, characterized by dogmatic assertion and a flimsy symbolism rather than by serious reasoning". I would hope to refute Eggeling's opinion.

I have simplified the material I have used, yet hope that I have not in any way presented it other than as distinctively Brahmanic. In order to make the rituals selected as representive as possible I have chosen three, the Agniṣṭoma which could be performed by any Aryan permitted to perform sacrifice, the Aśvamedha which could be performed only by a *rājā*, and the Agnicayana which was performed by a *brāhmaṇa*.

My third objective was to demonstrate the creativity of the *brāhmaṇas* in their use of the Prajāpati Creation/Salvation myth as a means of re-interpreting the Agnicayana of the Yajurveda, and in their use of material objects as bearers of symbolic meaning. An analysis of the altar design will show that individual graphics combined to make the plan of the altar, and that these same graphics form the *yāntric* patterns familiar in Hinduism and Buddhism.

My fourth objective was to show that, through the ritual, the *brāhmaṇas* were concerned with death, immortality, and the relationship of man to divine reality. Before the Brahmanic period was closed, and as a result of Brahmanic speculation upon ritual, the after-life with Yama had been questioned as man's ultimate objective. In the sacrificial system of the Śatapatha Brāhmaṇa, immortality became the reward of only a limited number of men, yet the doctrine of re-incarnation was formulated, and the theistic system of the Ṛgveda and the Yajurveda, which had characterized the ritual system, was rivalled by a different philosophy. This philosophy found expression in the Śatapatha Brāhmaṇa itself before it entered the period of the Upaniṣads as the Brahman-Ātman relationship.

In the end I might add that in analysing the contents of the ritual I have used as comparative material the collection of knowledge arising from ancient and modern literature, speculative theories relative to sacrifice and its origin and role in society, and ethnographic and archaeological data. I have especially drawn upon the insights of Jungian psychology in the field of archetypes and symbols.

ACKNOWLEDGEMENTS

I should like to take this opportunity of expressing my thanks to the following Authors and Publishers who have granted me permission to use copyright material from their works:

H. R. Ellis Davidson *Gods and Myths of Northern Europe* reprinted by permission of Penguin Books Ltd., England.

Joseph Campbell *The Masks of God. Vol II Oriental Mythology* reprinted by permission of Souvenir Press Ltd., London and The Viking Press Penguin Inc., New York.

G. B. Compton "The Cult of Sun Worship in the Rigveda".

R. C. Dutt *A history of Civilisation in Ancient India* reprinted by permission of J. M. Dent and Sons Ltd., London.

John Dowson's *A Classical Dictionary* reprinted by permission of Routledge and Kegan Paul Ltd., London.

Lakshmi Narasimha Somayajulu "A Protest Against the Torture of Animals at Religious Sacrifices : An Appeal to the British Raj and the Aryan Community" reprinted by permission of the British Library.

K. S. Macdonald *Sacred Books of the East, Examined and Described* reprinted by permission of the British Library.

Bal Gangadhar Tilak *Orion—or Researches into the Antiquity of the Vedas* reprinted by permission of the British Library.

A. A. Macdonell *A Vedic Reader for Students* and *A Vedic Grammar* reprinted by permission of Oxford University Press.

Heinrich Zimmer *Myths and Symbols in Indian Art and Civilization* ed. Joseph Campbell, Bollingen Series VI, copyright 1946 by Princeton University Press, copyright (c) renewed 1973 by Princeton University Press. Reprinted by permission of Princeton University Press.

Swami Prabhavananda and Frederick Manchester *The Upanishads : Breath of the Eternal* reprinted and translated by permission of Swami Amohananda, Vedanta Society of Southern California.

Juan Mascaro *The Upaniṣads* reprinted by permission of Penguin Books, England.

N. Macnicol translation of RV. X. 121.1 reprinted by permission of The Clarendon Press, Oxford, England.

Julius Eggeling translation of the Śatapatha Brāhmaṇa (SBE Volumes 12, 26, 41, 43 and 44). M/s Motilal Banarsidass, Delhi.

A. C. Bose *Hymns from the Vedas* Asia Publishing House, Bombay.

NOTE ON TRANSLITERATION OF SANSKRIT WORDS

When not quoting, I have transliterated as per E.D. Perry, *A Sanskrit Primer* (New York and London: Columbia University Press, 4th ed. 9th printing, 1965), except that I have transliterated श् as ś, following the Rev. Dr. Fulcher and Dr. Hauri, University of Queensland.

When quoting, I have reproduced the transliteration as in the quotation. This has made J. Eggeling's transliteration difficult to quote, since the printer has used varying forms of print (for example, two forms of the letter "s") to transliterate Sanskrit letters. Therefore, when quoting directly from Eggeling's translation, I have simply written s, k, g, or n.

ABBREVIATIONS

Ait. B.	Aitareya Brāhmaṇa
cf.	compare
ed.	edited by/edition
ff.	following
fn.	foot-note
imp.	impression
Intro.	Introduction
p.	page
pp.	pages
pts.	parts
R.V.	Ṛgveda
Ś. B.	Śatapatha Brāhmaṇa
trans.	translation
Vol.	Volume
Y. V.	Yajurveda

CONTENTS

CHAPTER I

SACRIFICE AND RITUAL

Introduction

My purpose is to extract from the heterogeneous and voluminous collection of ritual, myth, symbol, and speculation which is the Śatapatha Brāhmaṇa[1]* details relating to three of the most significant sacrifices and then to present those details coherently so that the reader may experience an immediate impression of the ritual. Having selected the material which appears to me to be the most significant, I have endeavoured to convey the distinctive personality of the ritual as Brahmanic ritual, by allowing the contents to be impressionistic so that they speak to the senses as well as to the intellect. After a lifetime devoted to the translation of the Śatapatha Brāhmaṇa into English, Julius Eggeling wrote of it as "of wearisome prolixity of exposition, characterized by dogmatic assertion and a flimsy symbolism rather than by serious reasoning."[2] I would hope to refute Eggeling's opinion.

Because I believe that any religious action should be considered as part of an equation the other half of which is divine reality—I have completed the thesis on a metaphysical plane by considering the concepts of divine reality inherent in the Śatapatha Brāhmaṇa.

In analysing the contents of the ritual I have used as comparative material the collection of knowledge arising from ancient and modern literature, speculative theories relative to sacrifice and its origin and role in society, and ethnographic and

*Numbered references and notes follow each Chapter.

archaeological data. I have especially drawn upon the insights of Jungian psychology in the field of archetypes and symbols.

Theories of Sacrifice: Comparative Material

Modern studies of sacrifice were made by Biblical scholars of Christian dedication who were interested in the meaning of sacrifice in the Old Testament because of its bearing upon the sacrifice of Jesus of Nazareth. The principal requirements of Hebrew animal sacrifice were written in the Old Testament books of Leviticus, Numbers, and Deuteronomy and the features of prime concern were: the relationship of the sacrifice to the god of Moses; the types of sacrifice to be performed; the choice of animals; the sprinkling of blood upon the horns of the altar; and details of the priest's share.

Attempts were made by the scholars to categorize types of sacrifice. T. H. Robinson[3] used examples from the Old Testament because they were "typical" rather than "unique", and from such material described the sacrifice of communion or peace-offering, the sin or guilt-offering, the wave-offering (named because the gift is swung towards the altar and then withdrawn), and the burnt-offering. E. O. James[4] theorized on the sacrifice which involved expiation and atonement. Since any misfortune or disaster is a sign of divine displeasure, the deity must be propitiated and the pollution expiated. Robertson Smith[5] proposed sacrifice as a communal meal shared through a kinship associated with totemism and his theory interested anthropologists when studies were made of totemism amongst the Australian aborigines. The destruction of the Temple at Jerusalem in A.D. 70 brought the Jewish sacrificial system to an end but when, in pursuance of Old Testament tradition, Jesus of Nazareth became the Paschal lamb, the final sacrifice of expiation and atonement for the Christian community, sacrifice in the Judaeo-Christian tradition had turned full circle for, in the Old Testament story of Abraham and Izaac,[6] the emphasis had been on the substitution of an animal for a human victim.

The archaeological discoveries in the Ancient Near East, especially the excavations of ancient grave sites at Ur by Sir Charles Woolley,[7] showed that a large number of people had been entombed with royal masters. This type of sacrifice did not fit neatly into any theoretical category and emphasis was placed on the general (religious) conclusion that the burials indicated a belief in an after-life, since the victims were thought to continue to serve their masters in death as in life. This custom of the living following the dead is known to have been practised in the twentieth century for, in 1912, the General Count Nogi, committed suicide at the precise hour of the burial of the Mikado, and his wife, the Countess Nogi, then killed herself to accompany her spouse. Although it could have been their intention that all would be reunited in an after-life, nevertheless, the emphasis was upon not being disunited in this life.[8] Joseph Campbell referred to this custom of the living following the dead as "the hieratic ideal of the mighty play"[9] and identified this type of sacrifice with the Indian *satī*, because of "the quality and character of mind and heart"[10] of the victims.

> For these sacrifices [that is, mass or single deaths following the passing of king or husband] are not properly, in fact, individuals at all; that is to say, they were not particular beings, distinguished from a class or group by virtue of any sense or realization of a personal, individual destiny and responsibility, to be worked out in the way of an individual life. They were parts, only of a larger whole: and it was only by virtue of their absolute submission to that in its unalterable categorical imperative that they were anything at all.[11]

It was customary in many Ancient cities to use the entrails of sacrificial animals for the purpose of divination and archaeologists discovered, in the Ancient Near East, a clay model of an animal's liver, with instructions in cuneiform, for the use of Babylonian priests practising haruspicy.[12] However, an animal used for such a purpose need not necessarily have been killed in a sacrificial ritual.

An influx of knowledge regarding tribal societies, made

possible by Western expansion to Australia, the Americas, Africa, and the Pacific Ocean, soon produced a generation of scholars who theorized endlessly—often by their own firesides—regarding the nature of primitive religion. Especially were they concerned with origins and precise meanings and with the significance of certain concepts, some of which were important to the development of theories of sacrifice, for example: totem, taboo, animism. Emile Durkheim[13] reaffirmed the communal eating of the totem as observed amongst Australian aborigines; Sigmund Freud[14] proposed that the first sacrifice arose from mankind's innate Oedipus complex and the associated taboo against incest (the sons killed the father, subsequently the totem, in order to possess mother and sisters); Edward Tylor[15] amplified his speculations regarding animism into his Embodiment Theory (the embodiment of spirits in man and nature and the possibility of the transference of soul from one body or object to another), a theory which would provide the rationale for the "scapegoat" sacrifice in the Old Testament.[16] Within anthropological studies Sir James Frazer[17] made a lasting contribution to the theory of sacrifice by collecting data relating to a dying god of vegetation, and demonstrated that there existed an ancient rite of royal sacrifice in which a king, in order to prove his continuing virility, seasonally accepted any challenge to his authority. The contestants fought to the death, and the victor's right to rule would again be subject to challenge at the end of a cycle. It followed, theoretically, that the virility of a king and the continuing prosperity of his kingdom were linked together; ritualized regicide therefore carried the greatest possible potency for the restoration of a kingdom's prosperity.

The primary motive of sacrifice had been thought to be *do ut des*—I give so that thou wilt give. This was rejected by W. Brede Kristensen as too simplistic, and he proposed sacrifice as a sacred and, therefore, mystical act. In relation to salvation-type sacrifices, Kristensen observed that the animal sacrificed usually represented the god, but could also represent the enemy of god, in which case the sacrifice was actually of half of the duality of god. For example, a pig sacrificed as Seth was actually the death aspect of Osiris. Such a sacrifice was viewed by the participants as death before renewal.[18]

When, at the turn of the century, Sanskrit documents began to be translated into European languages a new dimension of knowledge could be added to the Biblical, Classical, Archaeological, and Anthropological evidence. A study was made by Hubert and Mauss in which they compared material from many sources and reached the conclusion that the Christian sacrifice and those from other cultures were similar. They further concluded that the purpose of the sacrificial victims was to avoid the death of the sacrificer himself when he confronted god, a type of thinking based on the old maxim that no man can see god and live.[19] Although neither conclusion was generally acceptable to the scholars,[20] Hubert and Mauss had demonstrated an awareness of the intensity of the sacrificer's religious fervour.

The theories suggested by the generation of scholars under discussion are summarized in the following Table, where the representative material is arranged according to:

i. The type or purpose of the sacrifice, and ii. The source (literary or. cultural).

1. i. A burnt-, peace-, or guilt-offering.
   ii. Lev 1.10: Lev 3: Lev 4.
2. i. Expiation and atonement.
   ii. Lev 11.6
3. i. A communal meal.
   ii. Semitic.
   i. A communal meal with totem animal.
   ii. The Arunta in Australia.
   i. A totemic meal following slaughter of father.
   ii. Hypothetical (Freud).
4. i. Self-sacrifice to follow dead ruler.
   ii. Ur: Japan.
5. i. Divination.
   ii. Cuneiform tablets.
6. i. In anticipation of a favour.
   ii. Sacrifice of Iphigenia to gain wind for the Greek ships.[21]
7. i. Ritual regicide for community prosperity.
   ii. Priest-king of Nemi (Frazer).

8. i. A sacred and mystical act.
   ii. Dependent on interpretation of any piece of evidence.

(To these types, purposes, and sources may be added the following as proposed by S. G. F. Brandon).[22]

9. i. Food for the gods.
   ii. The Gilgamesh Epic.
10. i. In confirmation of a Covenant.
   ii. Yahveh's covenant with Israel: Ex 24.4 ff.
11. i. Offered apotropaically to ward off evil.
   ii. Blood on lintel prior to first Passover: Ex 12.3.
12. i. Made to, or for, the dead.
   ii. Funeral rites for Patroklos in Iliad xx, iii.166 ff.

The foregoing theories have not exhausted the interpretative possibilities in the sources available. For example, in Nordic mythology, Odin hung nine days and nights on a tree in order to gain a knowledge of the runes.

I know I hung
on the windswept Tree,
through nine days and nights.
I was stuck with a spear
and given to Odin,
myself given to myself. . .[23]

Gods, or animals symbolic of gods, were often sacrificial victims, but Odin was victim, the sacrificer, and the god to whom offered—as though there were an abstract, in the form of a Cosmic Omniscience, in which even a god may sacrificially participate.

The ritual suicide of a Japanese warrior in a temple is a second example of sacrifice for which the categories are not adequate. Such a sacrifice was described by an eye-witness[24] who emphasized the dignity of the condemned man as he seated himself and took up his weapon. The self-wound was a ritualized pattern, a deep stab to the left side and the blade then drawn across the stomach. The victim accepted, even welcomed, the presence of the witnesses one of whom could then deal him a death blow by severing the victim's head from his body.

This is a sacrifice to the social order rather than to a deity and again it suggests an abstract, this time of Perfect Man/Perfect Society.

A third example is the Aztec sacrifice of warrior prisoners.[25]

> The victims (twenty thousand) were prisoners of war. They were lined up, apparently unresisting, waiting to be spread-eagled on the sacrificial stone. The sacrifice's heart was cut from his living body and deposited in the heart urn of the Chac-mool figure. The priests immediately reached for the next victim.

Since there was no communal meal, this sacrifice does not belong in that category. Brandon regarded it as a sacrifice for the maintenance or renewal of life,[26] yet the sacrificers were not merely sustaining a deity but were sustaining the Sun—upon whose continued well-being our entire Universe does actually depend. Was this an offering to an Abstract Law of the Universe?

Diverse, both chronologically and culturally, as these examples are, they have two important elements in common:

Firstly, the victims were intellectually aware of the position and understood, even acquiesced in, their Fate—as if participating in some cosmic drama.

Secondly, all participants share an elementary belief that a situation exists which is out-of-season (a god not yet omniscient, a social role dishonoured, the sun losing strength) and that this situation can be righted on earth by a cosmic intervention which will be stimulated by the sacrifice. If the sacrifice has one constant element, it is man's belief that a conjunction in time of himself, the sacrificed, the deity and/or abstract, will influence the cosmos and man's position in it. These examples affirm the presence in a sacrifice of a nebulous quality not readily placed within the limitations of accepted theories and categories.

Ritual

When Freud applied his psycho-analytical method to a study of totem[27] he proposed that ritual came into being as a re-presentation of a previous action of which the emotional stress was so burdensome that it could only be released by repetitive action.

C. G. Jung applied his psychology to the ritual of the Catholic Mass and demonstrated, by the comparative study of symbols and archetypes, the importance of the influence of the collective unconscious upon mankind's selection of ritual actions.[28] Brandon supposed the "origin of ritual to be instinctive rather than rationally conceived."[29] Mircea Eliade observed the eternal return to the source[30] as when the Australian aborigine returns to the Dreamtime by means of ritual. Therefore, the source of the primary experience which originates a ritual form may be within or without man, but when expressed in perpetuation it is by means of symbols arising from an unbearable emotion, from the archetypes of the collective unconscious, from deep-seated instincts, or from reminiscences of a golden age.

The practice of ritual is "the prescribed order of religious service"[31] and "the form of activity, determined by consideration of tradition and symbolism."[32] It may be described as a re-celebration or re-enactment of a social or personal traumatic experience through which something significant to man of a spiritual or creatively intuitive nature exploded into human consciousness. The ritual continued to be enacted by successive generations because of tradition and because the symbols evoked an emotive response. It is certain that no individual sacrificer would have described his own experience in the analytical manner suggested but, if his rationale were that there is an interplay between his own mental and physical and spiritual environment and the natural forces in the universe, then modern creative science would have to agree with him. Even his belief that certain actions on his part could alter drastically his own environment, or influence the universe at large, cannot be discredited in this century.

No intensive study of ritual could be made until, between 1882 and 1900 two Sanskrit documents, manuals of ritual and commentary *to be used by the priests* who presided over sacrifice for the Aryan people, were translated into English. I refer to Ralph H. Griffith's translation of the Yajurveda and Julius Eggeling's translation of the Śatapatha Brāhmaṇa.

The Vedic *ṛṣis* had composed four Vedas or Books of Knowledge, the most important being the Ṛgveda. It was the third Veda, the Yajurveda, which Griffith translated in 1899.

This treatise had been intended for the Adhvaryus and consisted of hymns and prayers to be chanted or spoken in conjunction with the actions to be performed. In translation, this book numbers 371 pages with explanatory notes. As the creative and spiritual impetus which had inspired the Vedas failed (temporarily) to renew itself, the priests who controlled the ritual began to dominate religious expression and a second manual, the Śatapatha Brāhmaṇa, was composed. This was translated by Eggeling and published in five volumes between 1882 and 1900. Although this Brāhmaṇa is mainly commentary or exegesis, in translation it takes more than 2,000 pages. From such a rough comparison of the volume of the Yajurveda with that of the Śatapatha Brāhmaṇa, it is possible to sense the intense concern with the ritual of sacrifice which had developed in the priesthood during the Brahmanic period.*

In the Yajurveda the priests recorded how to perform a ritual; in the Śatapatha Brāhmaṇa they attempted to explain why. Unfortunately their manner of presentation often places a difficult barrier between the word and the reader. Because over the centuries changes in language, meaning, and ideas have taken place, the barrier can be insurmountable, but usually sufficient coherency remains to make the patient reader aware of the complexities and subtleties of Brahmanic thought.

So the question : WHY a ritual of sacrifice? One simple answer must be that it obtained satisfactory results. The ritual had worked in the past; the same actions performed in the present must gain similar results. One can observe the priests labouring, action by action, precisely placing a blade of grass this way, facing a piece of wood that way, almost in a state of terror lest a detail be altered or overlooked, and it is necessary to assume from this overwhelming preoccupation with detail and a sort of an "eye for an eye" philosophy about it, that the

*A difficulty has arisen in differentiating meanings for words derived from √*bṛh*. I have used Brāhmaṇas to denote literature and period; Brahmanic as an adjective referring to literature, period, thought; Brahmin as a special priest; and *brāhmaṇas* collectively and individually to denote caste. Since I believe it was possible to be an influential *brāhmaṇa* without being a priest, I consider that the *brāhmaṇas* may have been responsible for much of the speculation.

majority of the priests were dogmatic ritualists. The dogma of the ritual was also its doom because fear of an error in the tedious, infinitesimal actions led to legends of unfortunate sacrificers whose ritual went wrong. One such sacrificer was the King of Keśin whose sacrificial cow was killed by a tiger. The king asked of his fellow-sacrificers what atonement there was for such an event.

> They replied: "There is no atonement for this; Khandika Audbhāri alone knows an atonement for it; but he certainly desires as much as this, and worse than this, (to happen) to thee." Swiftly, the king decided. "Charioteer, put to my horses; I shall drive thither; if so be he will tell me, I shall succeed (with my sacrifice); if he will have me die, I shall be shattered along with the shattered sacrifice."
>
> XI, 8.4, 1 and 2.*

Ritual performed with such concern for correctness shows a neurotic concern with maintaining the correctness of outward signs. When ritual reaches this stage, it must perish or renew itself. I believe this climax was faced by the *brāhmaṇas* at the time of the Śatapatha Brāhmaṇa.

Brahmanic Sacrificial Ritual

At some time during the Vedic-Brahmanic period of Indian History the caste system appeared in a tangible form. The four castes are named in Ṛgveda X. 90, but in only one passage.[33] The Yajurveda refers to the castes by the repetition of the same hymn, and to the "five-classed" (Y.V., XXV, 23) and to the "races five" (Y.V., XXVI, 9) which were thought to be references to the four castes and the Niṣādas, or aboriginal tribes.[34] The four castes are named in I, 1.4.12.

At the Upanayana (XI, 5.4.1 ff)—though not necessarily at this early date—the sacred thread was conferred on those who were privileged to study the sacred texts. Whilst reciting Y.V. IV, 10, the sacrificer bound on himself a girdle of two plaited strands of hemp and one strand of Muñja grass.[35] In II, 4.2.1 the gods approach "being properly invested with the sacrificial

*All references are to the Śatapatha Brāhmaṇa unless designated otherwise.

cord" and the fathers approach "wearing the cord on the right shoulder" (II, 4.2.2). The ordinary manner was to wear the sacrificial cord on the left shoulder and under the right arm, but in any performance connected with the deceased ancestors, the cord had to be reversed so that it went over the right shoulder and under the left arm.[36] Thus, in II, 4.2.9 the sacrificer is described as wearing the sacrificial cord on his right shoulder. Therefore, whilst the full elaboration of the caste system in a social sense may be in the future, in a religious sense the right to perform rituals was being restricted to those entitled to be initiated at the Upanayana or to wear the Yajñopavīta, and it would seem that the ceremonial and sacrificial threads were identical.[37]

The Śatapatha Brāhmaṇa restricted the right to sacrifice to the three upper castes.

> Not everyone may enter it [a specially constructed shed or hall on the sacrificial ground] but only a Brāhman, or a Rāganya, or a Vaisya, for these are able to sacrifice.
>
> (III, 1.1.9)

Therefore, a man's right to perform, or to have performed, certain rituals depended on his social status at birth,* and the rituals performed by men born so advantageously were:

1. *Household rites*:
   Daily milk offerings; Agnihotra.
   New and full moon sacrifices: Darśapūrṇamāsa-iṣṭi.
   Establishment of sacred fires: Agnyādhāna.
   Oblations of cakes to ancestors: Piṇḍapitṛyajña.

2. *Community rites* :
   Offering of first fruits: Āgrayaṇeṣṭi.
   Soma rites.
   Funeral rites.

If, between the time of his marriage and his death, a man took seriously the sacrificial requirements of his religion, and yet never performed a major sacrifice, his sacrificial time-table for one lunar month would be:

*Please see note 53.

Daily: Morning and evening libations.

At new moon: The Agnyādhāna, or the establishment of the sacred fire if newly married; or the inauguration of the Darśapūrṇamāsa-iṣṭi which would be continued for thirty years or a life-time.

At full moon: The Darśapūrṇamāsa-iṣṭi was repeated and the sacrificer might participate in a harvest festival or make seasonal offerings.

Dark of the moon: Offerings were made to the ancestors.

Therefore, in any given month, the ordinary householder devoted many hours to his sacrificial obligations.[38]

There were specific rituals which were exclusively the property of the two upper castes. At the beginning of the Upanayana the initiator asked the student his name, obviously seeking his genealogy, as shown in the story of Satyakāma.[39] The Puruṣamedha could be performed by a *brāhmaṇa* or *kṣatriya*,[40] but even then note this injunction:

> But, indeed, this (sacrifice) is not to be imparted to any and everyone, lest one should impart everything to any and everyone, for the Purushamedha is everything; but one may only impart it to one who is known to him, and who is versed in sacred writ, and who may be dear to him, but not to any and everyone. XIII, 6.2.20

The Vājapeya was noted for the chariot-race in which the sacrificer, who must be either of the royal or priestly order, is allowed to carry off the palm.[41]

Two rituals, by their very nature, must have been exclusive to the *kṣatriyas*—the Rājasūya, the inauguration of a *rājā*, and the Aśvamedha, in which the principal sacrificer, because of the accoutrements of the sacrifice, could only be a powerful and wealthy *rājā*.

The Bṛhaspatisava—the inauguration of the *purohita*—was automatically restricted to the *brāhmaṇas*, as was the Agnicayana, not only because only a *brāhmaṇa* should perform it, but because the fruits of the sacrifice could only accrue to the sacrificer once in a lifetime, the implication thus being that no *brāhmaṇa* would perform it for another man.

That the needs of the ritual were complex can be seen from the following list of some of the implements the sacrificer may need:

- A spade of bamboo
- Tiger skin
- Skin of a he-goat
- Bee
- Cushions
- Elephant
- Ghee
- Sacrificial spoon
- Gold stool
- Ladder
- Milk and milking bowl
- Needles of copper, gold, and silver
- Strainer made of goats-hair and sheepswool and woven with gold
- Pressing stones
- Razor of copper
- Sickle
- Tortoise
- Seeds of herbs
- Black antelope skin
- Skin of a black deer
- Cart
- Drums
- Frog
- Gold in many forms
- Slaughtering knives of copper and iron
- Lotus flower and plant
- Mortar and pestle
- Ointment
- Bow and arrow
- Pearls
- Plough
- Porcupine
- Rattan mat
- Salt
- Shoes of boar-skin
- Silver plates
- Wheat used as headpiece for sacrificial post

That the society was complex may be seen from the roles of participants in the Rājasūya. Since this was a ceremony for a *rājā* it was supervised by the *purohita*. Part of the ceremony required that the *rājā*—accompanied by his *purohita* and attended by both retinues—should visit members of the court and at each household make a gift offering, thus:

At the house of	*the rājā made a gift of*
The commander of the army	Gold
The *purohita*	A white-backed bull

The king himself	A bull
The queen	A milch cow
Court minstrel and chronicler	A horse
The headman	A spotted bull
The chamberlain	A reddish-white draught bull
The Charioteer	Twin bullocks
Keeper of the dice and the huntsman	A dice-board a claw-shaped knife.
The courier	Bow, quiver, and a red turban
Discarded wife	Black, decrepit, diseased cow

(V, 3.1.1 ff)

One wonders if the wives were unaware—until the *rājā's* herald knocked on the door—who would be singled out and so ceremoniously and publicly discarded. There appears to be an appropriateness about the gifts generally as, for example, the keeper of the dice received a dice-board. On the other hand one would expect the courier to receive a horse. The gifts may have been similar to heraldic designs, so that the gift was in fact a confirmation of a tenure of office. A ceremonial sword was passed from *rājā* to kinsman, thence to court officials, each taking an oath of allegiance as in the hierarchical system of Europe's feudal age—that is, the second man owed allegiance to the *rājā*, and the third man to the second, and so on down the line. Other accoutrements required were a lion's skin, plates of gold, special robes, three special arrows. There was nothing elementary about a society whose life style was composed of so many social roles and whose possessions were so diversified.

There were also many specialist roles within the priesthood, the most important being: Udgātṛ, Hotṛ, Adhvaryu, and Brahmin. The Udgātṛ chanted the Sāmaveda hymns. In the early period the Hotṛ was both chanter and sacrificer but later he summoned the gods to participate in the sacrifice.[42]

There is an example of the gods being summoned in III, 8.3.33. The Hotṛ is "the voice of the sacrifice" (XII, 8.2.23) and he relates the Pāriplava Legend in the Aśvamedha (XIII, 4.3.2). In the Yajurveda the Adhvaryu performed the practical actions of the rituals and continued this function in the Śatapatha Brāhmaṇa. Since Bṛhaspati was the Brahmin-priest of the gods, and the representative and impersonation of the human priesthood,[43] we would expect that the Brahmins initiated any prayers personally applicable to the sacrificer. The Brahmin was to recite the Apratiratha hymn (as Bṛhaspati's representative) (IX, 2.3.1 and 5). Nevertheless, his function generally appears to be that of instigator, organizer, and overseer.

Each of these specialists was assisted by as many extras as the sacrificer could afford, for each priest was paid a fee, the *dakṣiṇā*. Although the gods accepted slaughtered animals as their portion, the priests liked to receive their fees "on the hoof." One thousand cows was a figure to a Brahmin's taste, but the cost of the *dakṣiṇā* and of the animals slaughtered must have been excessive and was unrealistic for the long term survival of any custom.

Along with these physical accoutrements of ritual, the Aryans were aware of a sacred dimension. This was especially evident in their careful selection of a site, which must be enclosed by specified boundaries so that only the priests, the sacrificer and his wife might enter there, and so that all objects not needed in the ritual might be excluded therefrom. Although some *ṛṣis* had expressed in their hymns the unifying experience of mysticism, and although the ordinary worshipper had a choice of thirty-three *devas* to whom to address his sacrifice, he chose to worship in high places so that there was an unobstructed vista eastward to the rising sun. By so orientating his sacrificial ground, the sacrificer did not mean to worship the rising sun.

The god Agni's attributes included those of fire and sun, the light of both, and the germination power of both. Savitṛ was often identified with the sun yet the hymns to Agni and to Savitṛ in no way suggest sun-worship. Uṣas as the dawn, the sun coming into being, inspired some of the most beautiful poetry, the *ṛṣis* representing her as a beautiful woman "her colour changing, who, doubly brilliant, displays her body from the eastward, and follows to perfection the path of Order, and, as one who knows all, strays not from the quarters" (R.V., V.80.4).[44] Whilst aware of the beauty of dawning light, the *ṛṣi* was seeing behind the dawn, and its daily repetition—a universal law.[45] Whilst I do not deny the probability that the sun was worshipped in Vedic times, I believe that the fact that the site was orientated eastward was symbolic only in the totality of conception, just as was the orientation of Christian cathedrals.

But such totalities become fragmented by the need for precise categories so that the East was the region of the gods (III, 1.1.2), the North was the region of men (III,1.1.2), and at the North-east, between the region of men and gods, was the gate of heaven (VI,6.2.4). The region of the Pitṛs was to the South (III. 1.1.7), and the West was the region of cattle (XIV, 2.2.28) and snakes (III, 1.1.7). As Hindu mythology developed, the arrangement became more complex with each point of the compass being thought of as the region or domain of a specific deity, who was assisted by an elephant to protect the gate of his realm.[46] A wrongly-orientated sacrificial site could therefore cause the sacrifice to go to a quarter other than that of the gods, and the presiding protector of that region would confer on the sacrificer the boons which were peculiar to that region. Such an unsought favour could be calamitous; a sacrifice, inadvertently tending towards the direction of the Pitṛs, would bring premature death.

The priests were aware of the need to ritually cleanse and sanctify the sacrificer. Before the ceremony proper the sacrificer and his wife went through a form of ritual cleansing in which water was used as an outward form for an inner shedding of sin and guilt (III, 1.2.10), although the text does usually imply a ritual uncleanness rather than a moral transgression. The wife must confess to the priest any extra-marital sexual intercourse (II, 5.2.20). After her confession, both she and her husband refrained from sexual relations for the duration of the sacrifice —from three days to twelve months. When holiness became intense, or purification from contamination essential, the sacrificer bathed and dressed in new garments (XIII, 8.4.6). And finally, to complete the sacrifice, the sacrificer was fully immersed in a stream so that he may be ritually desanctified and prepared for his return to normal life.

The symbolic use of water which cleanses the spirit and soul as it cleanses the body has been part of the ritual of many religions; the baptismal water of Christianity is water blessed and purified by the power of Christ in the priest. We gain some idea of the intensity and intricacy of Brahmanic ritual by the manner in which water was collected for the consecration in the Rājasūya.

> He first takes (water) from the (river) Sarasvatī. He steps into the water causing two waves to flow. He catches up water from the one in front, and water from the one which rises behind him... he then takes such water as flows against the stream of the flowing water... water that flows off the main current... he then takes sea-water... water from a whirlpool... water from the sunny spot in a pool... catches rain water while the sun shines . . . water from a pond . . . water from a well . . . he then takes dew-drops . . . he then takes honey . . . he then takes embryonic waters of a calving cow . . . takes . . . milk, clarified butter, moist sun-motes.
>
> (V,3.4 passim)

In collecting so many varieties of water, the priests collected the vigour and the essence of the waters. The water was not made "holy" by depriving it of its mundane qualities, but its properties were enriched and its efficacy increased by the moulding of diversity into one.

The priests abhorred the slaughter of animals and, despite the fact that to sacrifice an animal was the core of the sacrificial system, the killing was usually represented euphemistically as, for example, "they quiet the animal" (XIII, 2.8.1), so it is not surprising that when mention had to be made of human sacrifice attempts were made to gloss over the reality. One human who nearly died as a sacrificial victim was Suṇaḥsepha.[47]

Suṇaḥsepha's father was a brāhmaṇa but was, nevertheless, very poor. The king, Hariścandra, was rich in wives but had no son. He prayed to Varuṇa for a son, promising that if a son were born to him, he would sacrifice that son to Varuṇa. The son was born but Hariścandra dishonoured his pledge to Varuṇa and the son grew to manhood. At that time he learned that he was to be a sacrificial victim and promptly left home.

When Varuṇa became impatient for the sacrifice promised to him, Hariścandra asked Suṇaḥsepha's father, Ajigartta, to sell him one of his sons. So Suṇaḥsepha was sold for 100 cows. When the four officials of the sacrifice were to tie Suṇaḥsepha to the sacrificial stake, not one of them would do so. Ajigartta tied his son to the stake and was another 100 cows richer. Yet again, when Suṇaḥsepha was to be killed, the officiating priests could not do it and Ajigartta was again 100 cows richer.

By now Suṇaḥsepha had decided not to die so complacently and he appealed to the all-gods, and they released him.[48]

Apparently no stigma was attached to sacrificing a son since both king and *brāhmaṇa* were willing to do that; the stigma came from the contamination of the blood-guilt caused by actually dealing the fatal blow. This legend was to be retold during the consecration of a *rājā* and, since the original story required the *rājā* to sacrifice his first born son to Varuṇa, it may have been a custom to sacrifice the first born until a *rājā*, powerful like Abraham, said "nay" to the practice.[49] The Brāhmaṇas recorded that human sacrifice was gradually replaced by substitute victims :

> At first the gods offered up a man as the victim. When he was offered up, the sacrificial essence went out of him. It entered into the horse. They offered up the horse . . . and then the ox, the sheep, and the goat. When the goat was offered up, the sacrificial essence went out of it. It entered into this earth. They searched for it, by digging. They found it in rice and barley . . . and as much efficacy as all those sacrificial animal victims would have for him, so much efficacy has this oblation of rice and barley, for him who knows this.
>
> (I, 2.3.6 and 7)

In the Puruṣamedha, which lasted for forty days, the main focus of attention was upon the victims who were tied in successive waves to eleven stakes. Representative types from all walks of life were chosen, so that to the ideal of priesthood would be consecrated a *brāhmaṇa*; to the ideal of nobility, a *kṣatriya*; to the Maruts, a *vaiśya*; to penance, a *śūdra*; to darkness, a thief; to hell, a man-slayer; to evil, an eunuch. The list of victims[50] is an extraordinary document and, although the association is reasonably clear in the examples cited above, it becomes more difficult to follow as the list continues: actor, chatterer, wheelwright, barber, door-keeper, a barren woman, a grey-haired woman, a leper, a gambler, a lute-player, a cripple, and so on. According to the priests this sacrifice was to attain dominion over, and identification with, all creation. Therefore it followed that all parts of creation, cosmic and earthly, must be woven into the sacrificial pattern; for example, the year, the sun, the gods, demons, metres of hymns, the divisions of society, and types characteristic of humanity. Also, in Brahmanic logic, the sacrificer attained an inexhaustible supply of each food by sacrificing varieties of food. Logically, by the sacrifice of different types of men and women, the sacrificer attained the qualities of the victims. The text of the Śatapatha Brāhmaṇa implied that the victims were reprieved at the last moment, and therefore controversy exists as to whether or not the sacrifices were killed. L. Renou[51] estimated that 166 victims were sacrificed in 15 waves of 11 victims, plus one more person. Eggeling quoted Sāṅkhāyana as stating that it was a genuine sacrifice with real victims.[52] Remembering the method of departure of Egyptian kings and the evidence at Ur, it would require very little shift of evidence to make this a sacrifice of the victims and of the sacrificer himself (the one extra person). The Sarvamedha (XIII, 7.1) required the sacrifice of all possessions before retirement to a life of austerity in the forest. This need for bodily mortification could have arisen as an acceptable substitute for mortally wounding the body, since these practices appear to court death.

Some 3,000 years ago a man steeped in Vedic knowledge would decide to perform a sacrifice. During the time of that performance he believed himself to be removed from his ordinary, mundane self; he emphasised this by adopting a mystical name for the duration of the ritual. Before the sacrifice he made his *vrata*, a vow to maintain silence at certain times, to abstain from most food and all sexual intercourse. It was an oath of dedication to the proper fulfilment of his sacrifice; when it was completed he would be released from his vow and at the same time he would relinquish his spiritual name and that "other" self. In the following chapters, we examine the contents of three sacrifices, as performed by Aryans according to caste.[53]

CHAPTER I

References and Notes

1. This thesis has depended on two works : Firstly: Julius Eggeling, trans., The Śatapatha Brāhmaṇa, Parts I to V, Volumes XII, XXVI, XLI, XLIII, XLIV, of *The Sacred Books of the East Series*, ed. by F. Max Müller, (50 vols.; 2nd ed: Delhi: Motilal Banarsidass, 1966). Secondly: Ralph T. H. Griffith, trans., *The Texts of the White Yajur Veda* (3rd ed: Banaras: E. J. Lazarus & Co., 1957).

In response to my enquiry at the Oriental Text Room, British Museum (1973) I was informed that no translation of the Ś.B. had been made since Eggeling's, his having been first published by the Clarendon Press in 1882.

2. Eggeling: Part I, Intro. ix.

Compare Renou's favourable assessment: L. Renou, *Vedic India*, trans. P. Spratt, p. 26.

3. T. H. Robinson, *A Short Comparative History of Religions*, pp. 8 and 9.

4. E. O. James, *Sacrifice and Sacrament*. Also *Origins of the Sacrifice*, and *Myth and Ritual in the Ancient Near East*.

5. Robertson Smith, *The Religion of the Semites*. Lectures vi to xl, and "Sacrifice", *Encyclopaedia Britannica* (*9th ed.*) cited by Emile Durkheim, *The Elementary Forms of the Religious Life*, trans. J. W. Swain, p. 377, fn. 36.

6. Gen. XXII.

7. Sir Charles Woolley, *Ur of the Chaldees*.

8. Joseph Campbell, *The Masks of God, Vol. II: Oriental Mythology*, p. 499.

9. Ibid., p. 500.

10. Ibid., p. 65.

11. Ibid., p. 65.

12. Basil Ivan Rakoczi, "Divination", *Man, Myth and Magic* ed. Richard Cavendish.

13. Durkheim Emile, *The Elementary Forms of the Religious Life*, Book 3, Part 2, Section 1,"The Elements of Sacrifice," pp. 366-392.

14. Sigmund Freud, *Totem and Taboo*, trans. J. Strachey, p. 141.

15. Abram Kardiner and Edward Preble, *They Studied Man* "Edward Tylor," p. 86.

16. David Phillips, "Scapegoat". *Man, Myth and Magic* (1970).

17. Sir James George Frazer, *The Golden Bough, a Study in Magic and Religion*.

18. W. Brede Kristensen, *The Meaning of Religion*, pp. 458-468 passim.

19. H. Hubert and M. Mauss, *Sacrifice, Its Nature and Function*, trans., W. D. Halls. The sacrificer wishes to approach the divine, but hesitates

because there are destructive consequences at work; when certain powers intensify they cannot be concentrated in a profane object without destroying it. Thus the victim is destroyed whilst acting as an intermediary to protect the sacrificer.

20. I regretted that some of the material cited by scholars writing early in the twentieth century was not available to me.

21. The story of Iphigenia was made into a play by Euripides: *Iphigenia in Aulis*. The story outline may be found in A. A. Guerber, *The Myths of Greece and Rome*, p. 192.

22. Samuel G. F. Brandon, "Sacrifice" *A Dictionary of Comparative Religion*, ed. S. G. F. Brandon.

23. H. R. Ellis Davidson, *Gods and Myths of Northern Europe*, p. 143.

24. Algernon Bertram Mitford Redesdale, *Tales of Old Japan* cited by J. Campbell, *Oriental Mythology*, p. 497.

25. Victor Wolfgang von Hagen, *The Ancient Sun Kingdoms of the Americas*, p. 101.

26. Brandon, "Sacrifice".

27. Freud, *Totem and Taboo*, p. 141.

28. C. G. Jung, *Collected Works, Vol. XI* (Bollingen Series 20). "Transformation Symbolism in the Mass."

29. Brandon, "Sacrifice".

30. Mircea Eliade, *Cosmos and History: The Myth of the Eternal Return*.

31. The Concise Oxford Dictionary (5th ed. 1964).

32. Vergilius Ferm, ed., *Encyclopaedia of Religion* "Ritual."

33. Griffith, *Yajurveda*, p. 311, fn. 11.

34. Ibid., p. 276, fn. 9.

35. Ibid., p. 32, fn. 10.

36. Eggeling, Part I, p. 361, fn. 1.

37. A. A. Macdonell, *A Practical Sanskrit Dictionary* "Yajna upavita."

38. The qualities of a virtuous wife included her participation as an assistant to her husband at the daily household ceremonies. *The Kama Sutra of Vatsyayana* Intro. F. S. Klaf, p. 92.

39. Chāndogya Upaniṣad (IV, 4) cited by R. C. Dutt, *A History of Civilisation in Ancient India*, (2 vols.) I, pp. 158-160.

40. Griffith, Yajurveda, p. 303, fn.

41. Eggeling, Part III, xxiv.

42. Campbell, *Oriental Mythology*, p. 191.

43. Griffith, *Yajurveda*, p. 14, fn. 12.

44. Translations of Vedic hymns, unless otherwise indicated, are translations by A. C. Bose, *Hymns from the Vedas*.

45. Compare G. B. Compton, "*The Cult of Sun Worship in the Rigveda*. (Unpublished thesis, University of Queensland, 1977), where the writer arrives at the conclusion that Sūrya is not another sun god (p. 70) but the sun-god, and that the course of the sun shows that order exists (p. 22).

"When the Āryans saw the sun, they also thought of their creative invisible gods, the beings who gave the sun its course." (p. 70),

46. J. Dowson, *A Classical Dictionary of Hindu Mythology* "Loka."

47. Eggeling, Part III, p. 95, fn. 1: p. 109, fn. citing Ait. B. VII, 13-18 as the source for Suṇaḥsepha's story.

48. T. Goldstucker, *Inspired Writings of Hinduism.* First published in an Encyclopaedia in the 1860's, p. 51.

49. I have made a comparison of Isaac and Suṇaḥsepha and the relationship of their non-sacrifices to the culture of their respective religious backgrounds in *The Vedic Rishi : A Comparative Study of Mysticism and Sacrifice* (1972) Honours Thesis published under the name Naama Drury: *The Vedic Rishi.*

50. Eggeling, Part V, p. 413.

51. Renou, *Vedic India*, p. 110.

52. Eggeling, Part V, xxxiii.

53. *A note regarding the performance of sacrifices according to caste*:

The Ś.B. III, 1.1.9 states that the right to perform sacrifices was restricted to the *brāhmaṇas*, *kṣatriyas* and *vaiśyas.* I assume, therefore, that any sacrifice which was not restricted to either the *brāhmaṇas* or the *kṣatriyas* could be performed by any member of the three castes.

The Puruṣamedha could be performed by a *brāhmaṇa* or a *kṣatriya.* (Griffith, *Yajurveda*, p. 303 fn.).

The Vājapeya could be performed by a *brāhmaṇa* or a *kṣatriya* (Eggeling, Part III, xxv), and although Eggeling indicates that viewpoints differ (III, xxv), he quotes Āśvalāyana (IX, 9.19) that "after performing the Vājapeya, a king may perform the Rājasūya and a Brāhmaṇa the Bṛihaspatisava."

The Aśvamedha would be performed by a *rājā* since he alone had the necessary accoutrements: mounted horsemen to follow the horse on its journey for territorial gains, and a minstrel of his own as opposed to the priests' minstrel. The final fertility rite between the queen and the horse can only make sense if it is thought to embody on a grand scale the fertility and virility of an entire nation. Ś.B. XIII, 4.1.2 states: "the Aśvamedha is the kṣatriya's sacrifice."

With regards to the Agnicayana, it is true that the evidence is conflicting. Both the Y.V. (XI, 81 and 82) and the Ś.B. (VI, 6.3.13) refer to the use of a different number of kindling sticks according to the sacrificer's caste. However, I am of the opinion that the Agnicayana was a priest's ritual, although this exclusiveness could have developed as the result of speculation regarding the sacrifice of Prajāpati.

In support of my viewpoint I would point out:

This ritual had a separate line of teachers, each passing the teaching personally to his successor.

Compared with the other rituals the atmosphere created by the overall pattern of this ritual is overwhelmingly "priestly."

Certain aspects of the ritual point to *brāhmaṇa* rather than *kṣatriya*. For example, the fire is taken in procession on a cart drawn by two oxen (VI, 8.1.1) not a chariot with horses; the land is planted with herbs and the harvest used for medicinal purposes (the *brāhmaṇas* not the *kṣatriyas* were the physicians); three animals were said to represent castes (horse=*kṣatriya*: ass=*vaiśya* and *śūdra*: he-goat=*brāhmaṇa*) and when these three animals are led back to the sacrificial ground the he-goat leads the way (VI, 4.4.12).

Eggeling suggests (IV, xxv) that the Agnicayana was followed by the Mahāvrata which "as a rule, was performed in connection with a sacrificial session (sattra): and since sacrificial sessions, it would seem, could only be undertaken by Brāhmaṇas who would at the same time be the Sacrificers ... and their own officiating priests, the Mahāvrata [and hence the Agnicayana which it was to follow] would thus generally, if not invariably, be reserved for Brāhmaṇas."

In Ś.B. IX, 5.2.12 there is a directive against performing the Agnicayana, or the Mahāvrata, or the Mahad Uktham for another person, with dire consequences for the *brāhmaṇa* who does not observe the rule.

In my opinion, sanctions had developed about the Agnicayana ritual which made it the sacrifice for the *brāhmaṇas*.

CHAPTER II

THE AGNIṢṬOMA : A SOMA SACRIFICE

If a man of the three upper castes wished to inaugurate a sacrifice which was more efficacious than the daily or seasonal sacrifices, and yet not so significant that only a *kṣatriya* or a *brāhmaṇa* might be the celebrant, his choice would fall on a form of *soma* sacrifice, possibly a simple one such as the Agniṣṭoma, "hymns in praise of Agni."* This ritual lasted three days, one animal was sacrificed, and three pressings were made of the *soma*[1] plant. The juice, extracted from the plant, fermented into a beverage suitable for libations to the deities, or for drinking by the priests and sacrificer. Soma was intoxicating for, according to Dutt,[2] it was the intoxicating *soma* which caused the break between the Iranians and the Hindus. Nevertheless, the period of fermentation was so brief (in this sacrifice, overnight) that the *soma* may have had natural hallucinogenic qualities.

Introductory Rites

A well-defined pattern of actions was to be performed by the sacrificer, his wife, and the attendant priests who normally numbered five. The duration of the ritual could be extended, but certain components remained constant and were necessary for ritual perfection. The site had to be chosen according to the usual regulations, but the sacrificer was especially cautioned to observe that the land rose towards the south so that the sacrifice could not "spill over" into that quarter, for such a happening would be an omen of early death, as we have seen. Yājñavalkya, an authority on ritual whose opinion was accepted in most of the Śatapatha Brāhmaṇa, said that all the earth was divine and, therefore, any part of earth may be enclosed to become a sacrificial ground (III, 1.1.4). The Brahmins added that it was their excellent presence which made the sacrificial ground sacred, and therefore the sacrificer should choose only the best of the learned Brahmins as his officiating priest (III, 1.1.5).

A hall or shed was erected on the chosen site and fully enclosed so that the sacrificer—like the gods—could be withdrawn from

*The minute details relished by the priests have generally been omitted in order to elucidate the major actions or themes. The rituals are rich in symbolism and wherever possible I have reproduced the *brāhmaṇas'* own interpretation of them.

the world. Since the gods communed only with the three upper castes, the sacrificer was forbidden to speak to anyone outside of these castes, except through an intermediary. The sacrificer made the shed sacred by grasping the chief post of the eastern side. From this post dimensions were taken for the *soma* altar and the *uttaravedi* for:

> From that post he strode three steps forwards (to the east) and drove in a peg, the intermediate peg . . . From that peg he strode fifteen steps to the right, and then returned to the intermediate peg and strode fifteen steps northwards. Again, from the intermediate peg he strode 36 steps eastward, and marked the centre of the forepart of the altar. From this forepart he strode twelve steps to the right, and then 12 steps to the north. The high altar was then raised at the forefront and fire transferred to it. (Precis: III, 5.1.1ff.)

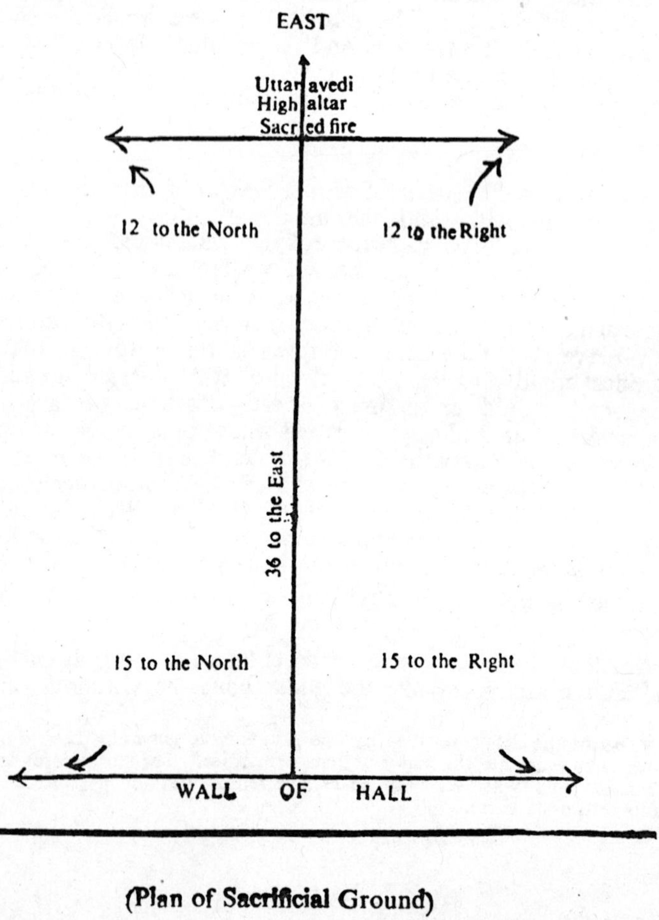

(Plan of Sacrificial Ground)

The sacrificer was prepared for his consecration by ritual bathing, shaving of the head and beard, cutting of nails, and the donning of a new linen garment. At the same time, but outside the hall, his wife was purified and anointed by an assistant priest who then brought her into the sacred area. The priests maintained their ritual purity by constant renewal, but especially were priests and sacred vessels cleansed and purified each morning of the sacrifice.

After the consecration the Audgrabhaṇas—libations to the gods—were performed. By these libations, the sacrificer elevated himself from the world of humans to the world of the gods (III, 1.4.1). The sacrificer then knelt on two black antelope skins and became, symbolically, an embryo: he girded himself with the sacrificial cord of hemp and Muñja grass[3] which the Brāhmaṇa describes as a "triple one" (III, 2.1.12) and received a staff for the warding off of evil spirits (III, 2.1.32). Having previously donned a new robe he has now, with the sacrificial cord and staff, received the three items conferred on the Brahmacārin.[4] Later in the ceremony he will emerge from his embryonic state. Could this be the origin of "twice-born"?[5]

The sacrificer remained in a position of meditation until sunset when he broke his fast with fast-milk. He prepared for sleep by praying to Agni:

> O Agni, watch thou well. May we take joy in most refreshing sleep . . . Protect us with unceasing care. From slumber waken us again.
>
> (Y.V., IV, 14)

And when he had passed safely through the night:

> Thought hath returned to me, and life; my breath and soul have come again.
>
> (Y.V., IV, 15)

The conclusion of this overnight vigil signified that the sacrificer had withdrawn from the world and had dedicated himself to the sacrifice; he was now in the hands of his priests—especially of the Adhvaryu, the director of ritual actions. Note how deeply involved are the sacrificer and his wife (on his behalf). The priests did not perform with the sacrificer as an interested bystander; they sold to him their knowledge and any influences, holy or demonic, which they invoked were the sacrificer's alone. For the time being they were *his* priests, concentrating their efforts on *his* needs.

The Animal Sacrifice

In order to cut the stake to which the sacrificial animal will be tied the sacrificer and an expert tree-feller enter the forest and select a suitable tree. When cut, the tree must fall in the right direction (eastward) so that the augury for the sacrifice will be propitious. The *brāhmaṇas* believed that the tree, as a living organism, participated in a spiritual life shared by all creation or—to express it with a different emphasis—that the tree was animated by living beings. The priests therefore made an offering of ghee (III, 6.4.15) in order to placate any hostile spirits who may have animated the tree and would now find themselves homeless.

The stake could be from 5 to 17 cubits long (cubit = 18 to 22 inches) depending upon the sacrifice for which it was required. For any length numerically expressed, the priests give a symbolic equivalent. For example, the stake could be 12 cubits long because there were twelve months in the year: it could also be 13 cubits long for the same reason (III, 6.4.17-26). Therefore, we have reason to assume that the *brāhmaṇas* were calculating both solar and lunar units of time. When the stake was erected, a goat was brought to it, and tied securely with the words :

> I bind thee with the noose of holy Order, thou offering to the Gods
>
> (Y.V., VI.8)

And then bound to the stake :

> By impulse of God Savitar I bind thee, with the arms of the Aśvins, with the hands of Pūshan, thee welcome unto Agni and to Soma.
>
> (Y.V., VI.9)

The animal and stake were then purified by the sprinkling of water, and the victim anointed on the forehead, shoulders, and loins. It was anointed on the forehead with the words "may thy breath unite with the wind" because "the breath of the victim when slain here passes into the wind." (III, 7.4.9) Compare the assessment of the *brāhmaṇas* that life departs with the breath with the Old Testament assertion that "the blood is the life" (Deut 12.23). Blood, though not seen in the Brāhmaṇa as the visible sign of life, did have potency. Grass was laid so that the spilt blood could fall upon it and spilt blood was the share of the *rākṣasas* to whom in "nethermost darkness" it was ritually discarded (III, 8.2.15 and 16).

Having completed their preparations for the immolation, the Brahmins withdraw and avert their eyes, for fear they should witness the actual killing. The slaughterer could either choke the animal by keeping its mouth closed, or strangle it with a noose.[6] Serene in their withdrawal, the Brahmins waited for the slaughterer to announce that the victim had been quieted, but "he must not say 'slay, kill' for that is human manner, but 'quiet it, it has passed away' for that is the manner of the gods. For when he says 'it has passed away' then this one (the sacrificer) passes to the gods, therefore he says 'it has passed away'." (III, 8.1.15)

The steps so far completed are what one would expect—the preparation of participants, the setting up of the stakes, the slaughter of the animal—these we have been conditioned to believe are the characteristic components of a sacrificial system. If we add to this the expectancy that the animal, or parts of it, will form a communal meal, we have the content even of eye-witness descriptions such as that recorded by the monks at Sinai.[7] But here in the Agniṣṭoma (not a very complicated ceremony in the Brahmanic repertoire) the rites subsequent to the slaying should dispel our simplistic views, for, the animal having passed away, the wife performed one of the many bizarre roles allotted to wives in the Brahmanic ritual. The Adhvaryu commanded his assistant priest, "Neshṭar, lead up the lady!" Obediently the Neṣṭṛ brought forward the sacrificer's wife, she with a vessel of water in her hands. With this water she cleansed all the openings of the body of the dead animal because it was thought that the vital airs, the breath, had departed from the victim through the nose, eyes, ears, navel, sex organ, and hind parts, and that the application of water would revitalize the animal (III, 8.2.6). Was it intended here that the woman plays the role of mother goddess, being attendant at rebirth as she had been at birth? When she had completed her ritual cleansing, the Adhvaryu and the sacrificer sprinkled the animal with the remaining water, partly to soothe any pain inflicted by the slaughterer, and partly to further restore the vital airs. The animal was then dissected and specific portions were cooked and offered to the gods, or ritually eaten by priests and sacrificer.[8]

This rather illogical sequence (killed, revitalized, dissected) was further confounded for the priests now touched the left-over portions of the animal, prayed over them thereby reuniting the parts, and again revitalized the whole body.

> In every limb is Indra's out-breath seated, in every limb is Indra's in-breath settled.
> God Tvashṭar, let thine ample forms be blended, that what wears different shapes may be one-fashioned.
>
> (Y.V., VI.20)

Having made the animal whole again the priests send it on its sacrificial way :

> Go to the sea. All-hail! Go to the air. All-hail! Go to God Savitar. All-Hail!
> Go thou to Mitra-Varuṇa. All-hail! Go thou to Day and Night. All Hail!
> Thy smoke mount to the sky, to heaven thy lustre. Fill thou the spacious earth full with thine ashes.
>
> (Y.V., VI.21)

Soma

Having dispensed with the animal the priests instigated a sequence of actions which would introduce *soma* into the ritual. A cow with special markings had been chosen as the cow to be exchanged for the *soma* plants and this was led towards the north where the *soma* merchant waited. The sacrificer followed in the seven footprints of the çow (designated by the right fore-print) and the sacrificer and priests sat about the seventh footprint, encircling it with a mark drawn by the sacred sword (III, 3.1.5). The dust of this footprint was gathered up and offered to the sacrificer and then to his wife, who received it with the words, "Thine, thine is wealth."

(III, 3.1.11).

Soma was not only a fermented drink but—as the plant personified or as the moon—a male deity. The wife was required to enact a rite which must once have been a fertility rite, but time had caused the original intention to be lost, or the priests had disguised it, for she was to be "looked at" by the *soma* cow. With the priests' penchant for euphemism and a reluctance on the part of the translators of the Victorian era to be specific about sex, it is not difficult to think of "looked at" as a sexual action, especially since the aim is a "productive union" (III, 3.1.11). However, the priests experienced a difficulty here since (obviously) both the wife and the cow were females. They overcame this by identifying the cow with the male deity for which it would be exchanged (III, 3.1.11) and thus the wife and the *soma*-cow were able to effect the desired union (figuratively).

A length of shining cloth was brought forward for use as the soma wrapper, and the priests approached the seller of *soma* and commenced bargaining. The exchange must have been pre-arranged, for it was performed like dialogue in a rehearsed drama.

> The priest asked, "Soma-seller, is thy King Soma for sale?"
> "He is for sale."
> "I will buy him of thee."
> "Buy him."
> "I will buy him for one-sixteenth of the cow."
> "King Soma, surely is worth more than that."
>
> The priest agreed that King Soma might be worth more than that, but praised the attributes of the cow. "Great, surely, is the greatness of the cow. From the cow comes fresh milk, from her boiled milk, from her cream, from her sour curds, from her sour cream, from her curdled milk, from her butter, from her ghee, from her clotted curds, from her whey. I will buy King Soma for one-eighth of the cow."
>
> "King Soma is surely worth more than that," countered the Soma seller.
>
> The haggling continued, the priest gradually increasing his offer until finally the Soma seller accepted gold, cloth, a goat, and a number of cows. The bargaining was concluded when the Adhvaryu passed a she-goat to the Soma vendor as the vendor passed to him the *soma* stalks.
>
> The Adhvaryu welcomed the *soma* : "Come to us, a

friend, bestowing good friends." The sacrificer uncovered his head, for now the *soma*, not the sacrificer, was the embryo.

(Precis : III, 3.3.1-12)

King Soma, regally wrapped in the shining cloth, was brought to the hall in procession. On entering the hall he was entertained as an honoured guest to whom the traditional Ātithya or guest-offering must be made. In this atmosphere of goodwill, the priests and the sacrificer made a covenant, the Covenant of Tanūnapāt, vowing they would not injure each other during the sacrifice.

The first pressing of *soma* was made in the morning . . .

Descend, O Soma, King, to all thy people. Down, unto thee, go, one and all, thy people!

May Agni with his fuel hear my calling. Hear it the Waters and the Bowls, Divine Ones! Hear! Stones, as knowing sacrifice, my calling. May the God Savitar hear mine invocation. All Hail!

(Y.V., VI.26)

The Vasatīvarī water, now called "Nigrābhya" because in the Hotṛ's cup (III, 9.3.30) was poured over the *soma* stalks which were then crushed between stones, and the liquid strained into special bowls. From this supply the priests offered libations to the gods, cup by cup. The words accompanying the libation from which the Agniṣṭoma was named were :

That man is lord of endless strength whom thou protectest in the fight, Agni, or urgest to the fray.

(Y.V., VI.29)

A second pressing was made at midday and a third in the evening. The gods were thought to gather about the sacrifice in eager anticipation, but only the *named* gods participated when invited to do so. Because of this, both the Yajurveda and the Brāhmaṇa have lengthy lists of the gods who may be invited, although the invitation was often couched in terms of epithets descriptive of the god's characteristics or functions (e.g. Y.V., VIII, 10 ff).

Major Themes of the Ritual

Since, compared with Brahmanic ritual on the whole, the Agniṣṭoma was a very simple ceremony, one would expect it to reflect the major theological concerns of Brahmanic theology rather than minor, segmented developments. Also, that these major themes would be prominent and concisely expressed because the priests had less time to entwine them with myriad minor themes.

One such theme was that the priests revitalized the dead animal. To my knowledge, the revitalizing of a simple animal-sacrifice is unique to the Vedic-Brahmanic ritual and such an action indicates a theological depth not usually attributed to ancient sacrifice. Logically, a sacrificial animal, killed, dissected, cooked, partially devoured, whose remains are rising in smoke to the sky is implacably dead. What, then, was the life to which the priests restored it ? Immortal life—they said—because immortal gods must eat immortal food. The *brāhmaṇas* here begin to theorize on their supposition that breath is the life and that it departs on the wind. This is one of the many indications of their preoccupation with the bodily signs which denote vitality, a preoccupation which arose because they were constantly seeking to identify that which was not mortal. Towards the end of the Brāhmaṇa, they were attempting to express their ideas on immortality other than as commentary on, or interpretation of, the existing ritual.

The ritual has also a tantalizing martial theme, explicit in the words of the prime oblation (above 32) which would have meaning only for a warrior. This theme is secondary to the cluster of ideas which surround the major theme, *soma*, as can be readily inferred from the following paragraphs which deal with that major theme.

In an introductory commentary Eggeling discusses *soma* as a divinity, and *soma* as the plant. With regards to origins he writes :

> The striking coincidences between the Vedic Agnishtoma and the Homa ceremony of the Parsis, pointed out by Martin Haug (Ait. B.I, p. 59 seq), leave no doubt as to the

complete development of the Soma-ritual in its essential features before the separation of the Indo-Iranians.[9]

Throughout religious history most rituals have required the drinking of some concoction as a sign of brotherhood (even the witches had their brew) and this concoction was usually introduced by a religious or spiritual figure. Tea-leaves were said to have developed from the eyelids of Bodhidharma when he sat for nine years facing a wall of the Shao-lin temple,[10] and the recipe of the liqueur, Benedictine, is still a secret of the monks of Fecamp Monastery. Since the priesthood was usually the medical profession, the most innocuous of drinks could be made stimulating by the addition of a suitable additive. There is no doubt that the *soma* was drunk for its exhilarating, mind-expanding, ecstasy-producing qualities.[11] To offer an experience outside of the normal to faithful retainers has often been the function of the priesthood but, inevitably, emphasis has been placed on the drinking of the *soma* and, again inevitably, this has led to comparisons with other rituals, notably the Bacchanalia, in which the sharing of a cup was a central rite.

Whilst comparisons with the Avestan and Parsi rites and inferences from Greek practice are valid, such comparisons have obscured other essential features: for example, the myth of Indra; the personification of *soma*; and the communal meals of meat and *soma*.

The *myth of Indra*[12] was taken for granted throughout the Brāhmaṇa (Indra actually slays Vṛtra in the thirty-fifth verse), and Indra was referred to in the Agniṣṭoma as the god above the gods: "the gods have Indra for their chief" (III, 4.2.2). All legends concerning Indra were basically variations on the same theme: Indra is constantly in battle with the Asuras and, whenever it seems that his strength will not be equal to the occasion, he drinks huge quantities of *soma* and in a *soma*-induced frenzy, overwhelms his enemies. Indra's myth has at least two major interpretations. The first is that of a symbolic battle, a conflict of opposites, since Indra's enemies, the Asuras, are (terminologically)[13] the fallen angels of Vedic literature. The word "Asura" once meant spiritual or divine and was used to describe Indra himself, but it acquired the opposite meaning "not a god," and became a term covering all opponents of the gods. Thus, in any duality, the Asura became the negative aspect, so that the god's attribute of order was matched by the Asura's disorder, good by evil, rain by drought, freedom by restraint. Especially Indra, as lord of the firmament, had an arch enemy, Vṛtra, who forever mocks him.

A second interpretation would make of Indra an ideal super-figure for a society who idealized the warrior, for Indra was "begat by a vigorous god and brought forth by a heroic female."[14] Magnificent in stature, brilliantly coloured, he drove a golden chariot, drawn by two tawny horses with flowing manes and tails. His weapons were the thunderbolt, arrows, a great hook, and net.[15]

As a war-god Indra bears comparison with Odin, the war-god of the Germanic peoples.[16] Both Indra and Odin were supreme in the sky. In the services of Odin was a dedicated group of warriors, the Berserks, distinct from the rest of the community as the *kṣatriyas* were in the Aryan situation.[17] Indra's perfect heaven was called Svarga, Odin's Valhalla. Dead warriors, or *those who died in a sacrificial rite*,[18] were taken to Valhalla by the Valkyries.

With regards to *the personification of soma*, the text reads throughout as if it refers to a human being. Soma is said to effect a sexual coupling with the sacrificer's wife: King Soma is bargained for by the priests (as Suṇaḥsepha was bargained for), King Soma is wrapped in a shining garment (royal robes?), taken in procession to the sacrificial hall, received as an honoured guest, and is present at the oath of Tanūnapāt; when he is about to die, King Soma is crushed between stones—the pressing skins of which were previously dyed red (to simulate blood?), and when King Soma is thus crushed the Brahmins say: "they slay him by means of that (stone)" (III, 9.4.8). That is, the slaying of Soma is not represented euphemistically.

Moreover, the ritual preserved the tradition that the *soma* was introduced from the outside, during the ceremony, by an outsider. Two questions need to be asked: Why did the priests not have their own supply of *soma*? Why was it not purchased before the ceremony as other ritual requirements were? The sacrificer was forbidden to converse with any person other than a member of the three upper castes, and the priests were fanatical in maintaining ritual cleanliness, yet *soma* came from outside.

And then, the *soma* vendor must be a *śūdra* or one of the Kutsa tribe. The *śūdras* were religious outcastes for, whilst theoretically the fourth caste and thus part of the Aryan society, in fact, they could not truly belong to it because they were not entitled to be ceremoniously invested with the Yajñopavīta. The position of the Kutsas is ambiguous. Kutsa was a Vedic *ṛṣi* persecuted by Indra; on the other hand, he was an ally of Indra in slaying the Dasyus. Indra and Kutsa were so alike that even Indra's wife could not tell them apart.[19] What associations the priests had in mind cannot be known, but it is certain that *soma* was introduced by people who were theoretically outside of the society, or under a dark cloud in their relationship with Indra.

After King Soma had entered the hall, the priests and sacrificer took an oath not to harm each other. An unusual precaution, for what had they to fear? The priests outnumbered the sacrificer five-to-one, so they had no cause for concern; it would not be priest-like to kill the goose that lays the golden egg, so the sacrificer had nothing to fear. In any case, the ceremony was half-way through. The only new component was that King Soma had entered, and for some reason his presence was a threat to the other parties.

There are *two communal feasts* in the ritual, that of the animal (III, 8.2.14) and that of the *soma* (IV, 2.1.29). There appears to be no evidence that the former was anything more than a communal sacrificial feast, that is, it does not appear to be a ritual eating of a slain enemy, or of a god. Eggeling described it thus:

> Whereupon the priests and sacrificer eat their respective portions; the straight gut being the Agnīdh's, the part above the udder the Hotri's, the *kloman* (apparently the right lung) the Brahman's, the pericardium the Adhvaryu's, and the spleen the sacrificer's share, whilst the Idā is eaten by all of them.[20]

On the other hand, the drinking of *soma* was described like a corporate communion:

> He then gives directions: 'Let thc Hotri's cup advance! Let the Brahman's, the Chanters', the Sacrificer's (cups) advance! Ye cup-bearers of the fire-priests, approach and fill up the cups with pure Soma!'—this is a composite direction. Having gone round (to behind the high altar) the Pratiprasthātri pours his residue (of Soma) into the Adhvaryu's (Sukra) vessel: whereby he makes the food pay tribute to the eater. The Adhvaryu pours it into the Hotri's cup for drinking; because the draught belongs to the utterer of the Vashat.
>
> (IV, 2.1.29)

In conclusion, I suggest that the Agniṣṭoma was a "refined" version of an ancient human sacrifice in which the Indra-Vṛtra myth was perpetuated as an Aryan-enemy rite. Little imagination is required to make the original King Soma a human being, an enemy king or warrior whose life was forfeited by defeat, and whose essence must be partaken of because of the belief that the partaking of the remains of a powerful man (or god) transfers his power to oneself. Because the victim had originally been an enemy the substitute, *soma,* was introduced from the outside. That the victim should be royally treated prior to death is a world-wide custom.[21] The victim had a second aspect, that of divinity, and in this the victim was either associated with Indra or Indra's enemy, Vṛtra, or possibly both. This is why the Kutsas, whose legendary founder was a mirror image of Indra, delivered the *soma.*

In the Brāhmaṇa, evidence exists in the form of cross-identification and analogy. When King Soma was ritually placed against the sacrificer's thigh the sacrificer—as of that moment—was Indra.

> Having pushed back the garment on the sacrificer's right thigh, he lays him (Soma) down thereon, with the text, 'Seat thee on Indra's right thigh'—for he, the sacrificer, is at present Indra.
>
> (III, 3.3.10)

According to the commentary, this was the position of a loved one and such an action would be suitable to the honoured treatment being accorded to Soma. I wish only to make the point that the sacrificer has been identified with Indra, but it would be interesting to speculate that this anatomically awkward position was also a symbolic gesture of submission since, whilst to occupy the right hand position of god or king is a place of honour, yet it also implies a position of inferiority in that it is not *the* central position.

We would expect the myth of Indra to contain references to Indra drinking his enemy's blood which, in a sense, he does for when Indra slew Vṛtra, Vṛtra flowed forth stinking in all directions. Strainers remove the Vṛtra-polluted water from the *soma* (I, 1.3.5).

Three times Soma was identified with Vṛtra:

Soma, forsooth, was Vṛtra. III, 4.3.13
IV, 1.4.8
IV, 2.5.15

It is precisely this cross-identification of victim and natural object, that *this* is an analogy of *that*, which we find in the "flesh and blood of the god" rituals in other cultures.

CHAPTER II

References and Notes

1. *Soma*: I have used J. Dowson: *A Classical Dictionary of Hindu Mythology* for a description of the *soma* plant as *Asclepias Acida*. Eggeling II, p. xxiv ff. compared the *soma* with the plant from which the present [1884] Parsis of Kerman and Yezd obtain the Hum juice, which they assert is the same as the Haoma of the Avesta. From the evidence, Eggeling agrees with Dowson that *soma* is one of the *asclepiads*.

2. R. C. Dutt, *A History of Civilisation in Ancient India* (2 vols.) I, p. 43.

3. Griffith: *Yajurveda* : p. 32, fn. 10

4. Dutt: *A History of Civilisation*, I, p. 263. "A garment, a girdle, and a staff of appropriate materials were then assumed by the student, and he approached the teacher."

5. cf. S. Radhakrishnan, *Eastern Religion and Western Thought*, p. 131.

6. Lakshmi Narasimha Somayajulu, *Pasu Vatha Khandanam or A Protest Against the Torture of Animals at Religious Sacrifices: An appeal to the British Raj and the Aryan Community* (British Museum Extract). "Several men, strong and able-bodied, take hold of the goat and shut all the openings in the body, such as mouth, nose, ear, and even the private parts and kick him and press with all their force and strength just as hammering on a piece of iron until the animal is dead (half-hour at least.") The author then claims that the sacrifices of the Veda were not real sacrifices, but were meant to be interpreted inwardly. Suṇaḥsepha was substituted for an animal, not a king's son. He quotes from the Vaiṣṇava Purāṇa, 3rd Amaha, 18th Chapter, 23rd śloka : "If an animal when sacrificed attains to heaven, why does the sacrificer not slay his father?"

7. A monk called Neilos wrote an eye-witness description of the sacrificing of a camel by a group of Arabs. Cited by R. K. Yerkes, *Sacrifice in Greek and Roman Religions and Early Judaism*, p. 79.

8. Griffith, *Yajurveda*, p. 56, fn. 22 says the heart was roasted and the stick used as a spit buried. Eggeling II, p. 209, fn. 1 lists portions for sacrificer and priests; III, 8.2.15 ff. lists portions for the gods.

9. Eggeling, Part II, p. xxiv.

10. Campbell, *Oriental Mythology*, pp. 441-443.

11. As an example of ecstasy induced from drinking see : W. K. G. Guthrie, *The Greeks and Their Gods*, Chapter VI, "Dionysos."

12. *New Larousse Encyclopedia of Mythology* Intro. Robert Graves, p. 326. The epithets and physical attributes of Indra were collected from the Vedic Hymns and used as introductory material for hymns to various gods, including Indra, by A. A. Macdonell : *A Vedic Reader for Students*.

13. The Indra myth was reduced to terminological terms by W. Norman Brown : "Mythology of India," *Mythologies of the Ancient World*, ed. and intro. by S. N. Kramer pp. 281-289.

14. Dowson, *A Classical Dictionary of Hindu Mythology*, "Indra."

15. Ibid.

16. Ellis Davidson, *Gods and Myths of Northern Europe*, p. 140.

17. Compare the Maruts who accompanied Indra.

18. Davidson, *Gods and Myths of Northern Europe*, p. 169.

19. Dowson, *A Classical Dictionary of Hindu Mythology*, "Indra."

20. Eggeling, Part II, p. 209, fn. 1.

21. Compare "they arrayed him in a gorgeous robe," (Luke 23:11) and "A superscription also was written over him . . . THIS IS THE KING OF THE JEWS." (Luke 23:38).

CHAPTER III

THE AŚVAMEDHA

By far the most exciting and spectacular of the sacrifices was the Aśvamedha, or horse sacrifice, which was performed by the priests on behalf of a *rājā* and was therefore a sacrifice for the *kṣatriyas*.

The Horse

Hundreds of animals were sacrificed at the Aśvamedha, but the horse alone gave its name to the ritual and perhaps the horse had once been the sole sacrifice. There were many positive reasons why a horse should be the central figure; its natural association with the warrior; its manifest virility; the importance given to it by the priests in their theological speculations; and because, in the images of the collective unconscious[1] man represented certain instinctual drives by an archetypal[2] horse.

In societies in which the horse has been a swift means of movement for warriors, it has become representative of knighthood, domination, power, and royalty. Where it is desirable to make such emphases in modern society, (e.g. ceremonial occasions) it is by the use of the horse that such traditions are re-created.[3] According to the priests "the horse corresponds to the Kshatra" (VI, 4.4.12) and the way in which their society reflected this belief is best illustrated by Buddhist legend. When Śākyamuni determined to leave the palace and seek Enlightenment, he left on his favourite horse, Kaṇṭaka, but, having travelled some distance to escape pursuit, Śākyamuni bid farewell to Kaṇṭaka and had him returned to the palace.[4] By such an action the Buddha-to-be symbolically rejected his role in society, in a manner which that society would understand. From that day onward the Buddha went on foot, for that was the practice of priests and holy men. In studying archetypes and the means of their symbolic expression, Jung found that the horse could represent the self, or the vehicle of the self, by which a man might make a transition from one state of consciousness to another. Again, the Buddhist legend is in harmony with this finding, for the horse was the vehicle by which the Buddha made a transition from one state to another.[5]

The priests believed the horse to be the mount of heavenly beings: "As Haya (steed) it carried the gods, as Vājin (racer) the Gandharvas, as Arvan (courser) the Asuras." (X, 6.4.1). The horse was known to the human world as "*aśva*." Because all but one of the horse's forms were vehicles for immortal beings, it followed that the horse knew the way to heaven (XIII, 2.8.1) that is, again, it was a vehicle of transition.

The priests said of the horse that it was born in the sea and that the sea was its kindred (X, 6.4.1). Jung suggests that wild horses symbolized the uncontrollable, instinctive drives which erupt from the unconscious (symbolized by the sea) and as an example cited a French film *crin blanc*, in which a boy on a stallion was pursued by assailants and finally cornered on the seashore, unable to escape, the boy and the horse swim out into the sea, and Jung interpreted this as an escape into the unconscious.[6]

Ideas such as these must have motivated the priests in their choice of the stallion which was brought forward to stand beside the *rājā* at the opening ceremony. The Adhvaryu placed about the neck of the *rājā* an ornament of gold, and the *rājā* proclaimed:

> Splendour art thou, bright, deathless, life-protector, Protector of my life be thou.
> By the impulse of God Savitar I take thee with the arms of Aśvins, with the hands of Pūshan. This girdle, which in their religious meetings sages assumed in earlier time of worship.
> Is present with us here at this libation, in the Law's hymn, proclaiming rich abundance.
>
> (Y.V. XXII, 1.2.)

(A girth of grass was then tied about the horse).

Famous art thou, thou art the world, controller and upholder thou.
Go, consecrate by Svāhā to Agni Vaiṣvānara widely-famed.
(Y.V., XXII, 3)

By this dual investiture was established the close association, if not identification, of sacrificer and sacrificed. The gods, especially Savitṛ, Agni, and Soma were invited to be present by the offering of prayers and oblations, and the horse extravagantly eulogized:

Mighty through thy dam, eminent through thy sire, thou art a horse, thou art a steed, thou art a courser, thou art a comfort, thou art a racer, thou art a yoke-horse, thou art a strong steed, thou art a stallion, thou art manly-minded.
(Y.V., XXII, 19)

Imagine the scene! The stallion was to be driven from the sacrificial ground in a north-easterly direction (towards the Gate of Heaven). Sensitive and wary, without the control of a rider, circling, rearing, plunging, he was forcibly driven away, for the purpose was to set him free, to drive him from familiar pastures into neighbouring kingdoms. As he finally galloped free, aquiver at the unexpected return to his natural kingdom, he was joined by an escort of one hundred princes, one hundred warriors with swords, one hundred bowmen, one hundred men armed with staves. For twelve months the stallion and his retinue would wander the countryside claiming for the *rājā* over-lordship of all lands into which the stallion wandered. The priests warned the departing escort :

Those who go on to the end of this sacrifice will become (sharers of) the royal power, they will become kings worthy of being consecrated: but those who do not go on to the end of this (sacrifice) will be excluded from royal power, they will not become kings, but nobles and peasants, unworthy of being consecrated: do not ye therefore be heedless and keep it (the horse) from water suitable for bathing and from mares.
(XIII, 4.2.17)

Because the pageantry appealed to the epic poets, the Aśvamedha was celebrated by Yudhiṣṭhira in the Mahābhārata and by Rāma in the Rāmāyaṇa. In the Rāmāyaṇa we are given a glimpse of what would happen if the horse did not return, or if its progress was barred by a rival unwilling to submit to the *rājā*'s suzerainty. Rāma's wife, Sītā, had been exiled but received protection from Vālmīki who composed the Rāmāyaṇa and taught it to Sītā's two sons, who had been born in exile.

> Then Rāma decided to celebrate the Aśvamedha sacrifice and sent out the horse. The animal came as far as Vālmīki's hermitage, and the boys, in playful humour, caught it and detained it. Rāma's troops tried in vain to recover the animal. At last Rāma himself saw the princely boys.[7]

We can see that Rāma was forced to attend in person and this was probably the usual pattern, that is, to challenge the horse was to issue a personal challenge to the *rājā* who had sent him.

The Pāriplava Legend

When the stallion and its entourage had departed from the sacrificial enclosure, the Adhvaryu placed a cushion of gold thread to the south of the *vedi* and on this the Hotṛ seated himself. The *rājā* sat upon a stool of gold, and on his right—also on gold-wrought cushions, sat the Brahmin and the Udgātṛ. About this group clustered all the people waiting to hear the Pāriplava legend. This was a cycle of teaching which lasted for almost a year, made up of mini-cycles, each of ten days. On each of the ten days the Hotṛ retold the myths and legends to the people, recited the beautiful stanzas of Vedic poetry, taught the spiritual traditions of the Vedas, talked of demons, witchcraft, magic, of poisons, and of cures. When the Hotṛ had finished for the day, a minstrel sang of the deeds of righteous kings of old, thus making the *rājā*-sacrificer one with the royal heritage of centuries.

> 'Masters of lute-players,' he says, 'sing ye of this Sacrificer along with righteous kings of yore!' and they accordingly

sing of him; and in thus singing of him, they make him share the same world with the righteous kings of yore.

(XIII, 4.3.3)

When the ten-day series of teaching was completed, a new cycle commenced—and in this manner the Pāriplava legend progressed throughout the year of the stallion's wanderings.

The First Day :

'King Manu Vaivasvata,' he [the Hotṛ] says*:— 'his people are Men, and they are staying here;'—householders, unlearned in the scriptures, have come thither; it is these he instructs: 'The Rik (verses) are the Veda: this it is;' thus saying, let him go over a hymn of the Rik, as if reciting it.

(XIII, 4.3.3)

The name, Manu, was derived from √ *man*, "to think."[8] Therefore, at the very beginning of their records, the Aryans have grasped the essential attribute of man. King Manu Vaivasvata was the son of Sūrya, the sun. Whilst in the forms of a horse and mare, Sūrya and Sañjñā (or a nymph called Aśvinī) procreated other children.[9] King Manu Vaivasvata's son was Ikṣvāku and from him—the grandson of the sun—the Solar race of kings traced its ancestry.[10] No doubt a genealogy existed by which the king for whom the Aśvamedha was being celebrated, could claim descent from Manu and thence from the sun itself, not in the sense of being an object in the sky—but in the sense of being dynamic, of having superior intellectual and physical power, and the aura of royalty and divine rightness. Rāma, of the Rāmāyaṇa, was of the Solar race. There was also a Lunar race descended from the *ṛṣi*, Atri.[11] The Kauravas and Pāṇḍavas of the Mahābhārata were of the Lunar race.

Manu was also the name given to fourteen mythological progenitors of mankind, rulers of earth, each of whom holds power for the period called a *manvantara* (Manu-antara), a

*This was the Hotṛ's pattern for announcing the subject of each day's teaching. Since the Ś.B. does not give specific content, I have supplied the content from other sources, but I have remained true to the subject heading by using only gods, heroes, myths, and legends referred to in the Ś.B.

period of 4,320,000 years[12] or 3067,200,000 years.[13] Because Manu Vaivasvata is the *manu* of the present age, the seventh, when the *brāhmaṇas* recorded the ritual of the Aśvamedha, they believed that the universe had existed in some form for over 25,920,000 years (ff Macdonald and Dowson) or 18,403,200,000 years (ff Zimmer) having gone through six periods of evolution and involution, of creation and destruction. The previous period of destruction had been caused by a great flood but Manu Vaivasvata had survived that flood to become the progenitor of the human race in the seventh age. The legend of the flood was recorded in the Śatapatha Brāhmaṇa:

> One morning they brought to Manu water in which to wash his hands. As he washed, a fish came into his hands. "Rear me", the fish said, "and I will save you."
>
> "From what will you save me?" asked Manu.
>
> "A flood will carry away all creatures and I will save you from the flood."
>
> "How can I rear you?"
>
> The fish replied that as long as he was small there was great danger for him, since fish devours fish.
>
> "Therefore, at first keep me in a jar. Then when I am too big for the jar, dig a pit for me. When I outgrow the pit take me down to the sea for I shall be beyond destruction."
>
> When the fish was very large Manu released it to the sea. Before leaving, the fish said, "In a certain year the flood will come. In that year, build a boat."
>
> So in the year predicted, Manu did build a boat and, as the water rose, the fish surfaced beside the boat and, after fixing a rope between itself and the boat, towed the boat to the northern mountains.
>
> The fish told Manu to fasten the ship to a tree for the present, but to gradually descend the mountain as the water subsided. The flood then swept away all creatures, and only Manu remained.
>
> (Precis : I, 8.1.1-6)

The priest whose charge it was to know the Ṛgveda now came forward to recite, and comment upon, a selected hymn. Since Sūrya was the founder of the solar race perhaps the priest recited this hymn of Vasiṣṭha.

Up rises the beautiful orb,
on the near margin of the sky,
as the divine white-coloured steed bears it fast
making it visible to all.

The Sun, shining on all, crest by crest,
the lord of what moves and what stands still,
the seven sister bays bear in the chariot
for the well-being of the world.

That eye, divinely placed, rising bright,
may we see for a hundred autumns,
May we live for a hundred autumns.

(R.V., VII, 66.14-16)

Then a minstrel told tales of old, perhaps of the eternal conflict between *brāhmaṇas* and *kṣatriyas* as in the story of the sage Vasiṣṭha (XII, 6.1.38) and Nimi,*[14] the son of Ikṣvāku, and founder of the dynasty of Mithilā, an important name high on the list of the Solar dynasty.

> Nimi was cursed by Vasishtha and lost his bodily form; not to be outdone, Nimi gave back the curse, and both Nimi and Vasishtha abandoned their bodily forms. Vasishtha was born again as the issue of Mitra and Varuṇa. "But the corpse of Nimi was preserved from decay by being embalmed with fragrant oils and resins, and it remained as entire as if it were immortal."[15]
>
> The gods were willing to restore Nimi to bodily life, but he declined, declaring that the separation of soul and body was so distressing that he would never resume a corporeal shape and become liable to it again. "To this desire the gods assented, and Nimi was placed by them in the eyes of all living creatures, in consequence of which their eyelids are ever opening and shutting."[16]

The theme of rivalry is overt, but note what was taken for granted: Nimi's dead body could be treated with herbs to prevent deterioration; Nimi had a soul distinct from his body;

*Nimi's "son" was Janaka (14) and his namesake and descendant by twenty generations is a prominent figure in the Ś.B. e.g. XI, 3.1.2.

that soul contained Nimi's entire personality and could have reanimated his body.

When the sun had set and the fires had been lighted, the *rājā*'s minstrels sang ballads eulogizing the *rājā* and his ancestors, of bravery in battle, of virility, of love of the arts, and perhaps they retold the story of this same Nimi, who had died without a successor. Unwilling to permit such a tragedy, the sages subjected Nimi's body to attrition, and produced from it a prince who was called Janaka, from being born without a progenitor.[17]

And thus ended the first day of the cyclic legend: the wonder of the beginning of things: a universe dissolves and re-emerges, the human race dies and one man lives, a king dies and yet lives, and a king's son is born other than through the womb.

The Second Day :

> 'King Yama Vaivasvata,' the Hotri says, 'his people are the Fathers, and they are staying here;' old men have come thither: it is these he instructs—'The Yagus-formulas are the Veda: this it is:' thus saying, let him go over a chapter of the Yagus, as if reciting it.
>
> (XIII, 4.3.6)

Yama was the first man to be born in the age of perfection, that golden age when all men attained a life of one hundred summers. Therefore, Yama was the first to die (X.13.4), the pathfinder to the afterlife, (X.14.2) and overlord of the dead. (X.14.15) In all probability, all elders of the community were the important guests on this day. On the first day the focus had been on men, on the third day it will be on handsome youths, and on the fourth day on young maidens. Each day throughout the Pāriplava legend a specific part of the community will be honoured.

It is significant that the elders (as incipient Pitṛs?) were honoured on the second day. Vedic philosophy was the reverse of the trite panacea "only the good die young" for the longer a man lived and the closer he drew towards that magical one hundred, the greater the proof that the gods favoured him. The *brāhmaṇas* eventually speculated that immortality comes from exposure to the immortal sun (below p. 111), therefore, the man who had lived many suns was closer to immortality than his younger companions, and he was venerated for his age. The priest recited from the Yajurveda:

> To Agni Hail! who bears gifts due to Sages. To Soma Hail! accompanied by Fathers.
> Expelled are Asuras and fiends who sate upon the covering grass.
> The Asuras, attracted by oblation, who roam at will assuming varied figures, from this our world may Agni drive them, whether they clothe themselves in large or little bodies.
> O Fathers, here enjoy yourselves. Come hither, like bulls, come each to his allotted portion.
> The Fathers have enjoyed themselves, and hither, like bulls, come each to his allotted portion.
> Obeisance to your genial sap, O Fathers! Fathers, obeisance unto you for Ardour! Fathers, obeisance unto you for Svadhā! Obeisance unto you for life, O Fathers!
>
> (Y.V., II, 29-32)

These were the words of the ceremony in which the elders would be honoured when death had claimed them. Ancestor worship is not worship of men, but, as is expressed clearly here, worship of life. Since one's life is a gift from parents, and thus a gift from the ancestor, this living thread must be honoured. "Obeisance unto you for life, O Fathers!"

The Third Day :

> 'King Varuna Āditya,' he says: 'his people are the Gandharvas, and they are staying here :'—handsome youths have come thither: it is these he instructs: 'The Atharvans are the Veda: this it is' thus saying, let him go over one section (Parvan) of the Atharvan, as if reciting it.
>
> (XIII, 4.3.7)

Varuṇa was the foremost of the six or seven sons of Aditi, the free, unbounded, infinite; the *ādityas* were the inviolable, imperishable, eternal beings. Varuṇa—in Vedic times—was a god with those qualities which mortals think of as god-like—unlimited power over nature and man; control of the universal laws which underlie creation; unbounded knowledge, especially of herbal medicine. The priests of the Brāhmaṇa respected Varuṇa's power to loose or to bind, especially the negative, binding power.

The Gandharvas were male, virile, beautiful, musical, a fitting retinue of messengers between Varuṇa and mankind. The Atharvaveda speaks of 6,333 Gandharvas.[18]

I am doubtful what traditional teaching belonged to this third day, but if the pattern set by the first and second day were followed, I would expect something from the Sāmaveda, although the Brāhmaṇa states that the teaching was from the Atharvaveda. Since the Sāmaveda consists of the hymns of the Ṛgveda rearranged,[19] it would be superfluous to repeat them, although this does happen on the tenth day. There is an appendix to the Sāmaveda called the Gandharva Veda,[20] the science of music and song, drama and dancing, and therefore a sacred drama and dance may have been performed on the third day.

The Fourth Day :

> 'King Soma Vaiṣhnava,' he says: 'his people are the Apsaras, and they are Staying here:'—handsome maidens have come thither; it is these he instructs;—'The Aṅgiras are the Veda: this it is:' thus saying, let him go over one section of the Aṅgiras. (XIII, 4.3.8)

Soma was the fiery, liquid *amṛta* of the gods and, in another aspect, the moon or moon-god. There is the obvious connection of the moon and tidal waters and all liquid forms in the world; including the watery percentage in the human body. Soma Vaiṣṇava means "moon of the sun" (*soma* = moon: Vaiṣṇava = of Viṣṇu, the sun) which appears to be such a contradiction in content that the phrase may be only an expression of natural fact, namely, that the light of the moon is the reflection of the sun. To contrast sun and moon is a traditional way of expressing poetically the eternally complementary roles of male and female and, although Soma was a male deity, the feminine associations are present in the goddess of the new moon (below pp. 79-80) and in Soma's retinue of beautiful maidens. Even without a sexual association, the sun and moon express the continuing dichotomy of all types of contrasting opposites: day and night, positive and negative, outpouring and receptive. Since this was the day of the beautiful maidens perhaps *rājās* of the sun-race ideally selected wives from the moon dynasty.

Poetically expressed the Apsaras were the vapours and mists which rise from the earth in response to the sun's intensity. One Apsarā, Urvaśī, had been loved by a mortal, King Purūravas (XI, 5.1.1).

Urvaśī was playing with another Apsarā when they were carried away by demons, but saved by king Purūravas. Urvaśī and Purūravas became lovers but she, on her part, insisted on two conditions. The first was that she should always have her two pet rams sleeping by her bedside and the second that she should never see Purūravas undressed.

The Gandharvas, who were normally the companions of the Apsaras, wished for the return of Urvaśī to Svarga. In order to make this happen, the Gandharvas one night stole Urvaśī's rams, forcing Purūravas to respond to her cries of distress by leaping naked from his bed. The Gandharvas then caused lightning to illuminate the naked Purūravas and he was seen by Urvaśī. The charm was broken and Urvaśī disappeared.

The disconsolate Purūravas sought her everywhere and finally found her as she swam amongst a flock of swans. Moved to pity by his devotion, Urvaśī agreed to a meeting on the night when their child would be born. The Gandharvas then offered to Purūravas the fulfilment of any one desire. He asked to live for ever with Urvaśī.

This presented a problem — how to make Purūravas a Gandharva — and the problem was solved by instructing Purūravas in a form of fire sacrifice.[21]

It is appropriate that man's learning to make fire, which is also the fire of immortality, should follow on teachings concerning a concept of Time matched in vastness by light years, of a universe created and destroyed, of the first man and the bond of life which links generation to generation. The components of this fourth day—*soma*, sun, liquid, fire—cling together as symbolic compatibles rather than in an ordered, intellectual fashion. The priest was to read part of the Aṅgiras and since the hymns of the Atharvaveda were called Aṅgiras, he may have continued the pattern by reading from the fourth Veda.

The basis of teaching for the first four days has concentrated upon the eternal or supra-normal, but on the fifth day there is a change of emphasis to the problems of man. The first emphasis was the practice of medicine, the second was the assault of man by demons and evil spirits, and the third the performance of magic in an attempt to appease the negative aspect of the gods.

The Fifth Day :

> 'King Arbuda Kādraveya,' he says: 'his people are the Snakes, and they are staying here;'—both snakes and snake-charmers have come thither: it is these he instructs;—'The Sarpavidyā (science of snakes) is the Veda; this it is;' thus saying, let him go over one section of the Sarpavidyā as if reciting it.
>
> (XIII, 4.3.9)

Arbuda was a serpent, the offspring of Kadrū, the mother of one thousand powerful, many-headed serpents. That day the priest taught from the "Knowledge of Serpents," a treasury of poisons and consequently of healing. The caduceus, which became the emblem of modern medicine, is a wand intertwined with snakes.

The Sixth Day :

> 'King Kubera Vaisravana,' he says: 'his people are the Rakshas, and they are staying here;'—evil-doers, robbers, have come thither: it is these he instructs;—'The Devaganavidyā (demonology) is the Veda: this it is:' thus saying, let him go over one section of the Devaganavidyā, as if he were reciting it.
>
> (XIII, 4.3.10)

Kuvera, the vile body, was a chief of evil beings and spirits, keeper of gold, silver, and all the metals of the earth.[22]

The Rākṣasas were evil-doers, robbers, and adept magicians. Some of their qualities may be inferred from their epithets: killers or hurters, stealers of the offerings, strong in twilight, night-walkers, cannibals, carnivorous, blood-drinkers, biters, gluttons, black-faced.[23]

The priest taught from the "Knowledge of Demonology."

The Seventh Day :

> 'King Asita Dhānva,' he says: 'his people are the Asura; and they are staying here;' —usurers have come thither; it is these he instructs;—'Magic is the Veda; this it is:' thus saying, let him perform some magic trick.
>
> (XIII, 4.3.11)

King Asita (black) was an aspect of Vṛtra. The Asuras typified the negative qualities of the "other," whose powers were carefully controlled by the priests during sacrifice. The Asuras, by way of witchcraft, buried charms of bones, nails, hair, and similar objects tied up in worn matting, somewhere in the sacred grounds in an attempt to overcome the gods. The priests dug into the grounds seeking any such charms which may have been secreted there by kin or foe who willed misfortune on the sacrifice.

On this day the priest had to perform a magic trick, or sleight-of-hand, but since the priests took an extraordinary interest in the power of numbers (and usurers must have a knowledge of arithmetic) it is possible that the priests exhibited some form of the magic square still popular in India today.[24]

Eggeling commented: "The association of the black art with the usurer or money-lender is rather curious."[25] I suggest that the attendants on these three days (snake-charmers, evil-doers, and usurers) may have formed the negative aspect of the community. This is especially clear where the usurers are identified with the negative aspect of Indra. The usurers may have been outside of the Vedic society, as in the case of the suppliers of the *soma* stalks. Compare the situation of the Jew as moneylender throughout the history of the Western world, and the humiliating roles often played by Jews during city festivals.[26]

The Eighth Day :

> 'King Matsya Sāmmada,' he says; 'his people are the water-dwellers, and they are staying here:'—both fish and fishermen have come thither; it is these he instructs;— 'the Itihāsa is the Veda: this it is:' thus saying, let him tell some Itihāsa.
>
> (XIII, 4.3.12)

This day brought a renewal of positive teaching. The priest was to relate from the Itihāsas, legends of gods and kings and stories of once upon a time. A king of the Matsyas called Dhvasan Dvaitavana (XIII, 5.4.9) performed the Aśvamedha after he had been victorious in battle. He dedicated fourteen steeds to Indra Vṛtrahan beside a lake which from that day was called Lake Dvaitavana.

The Ninth Day :

> 'King Tārkshya Vaipasyata,' he says; 'his people are the Birds, and they are staying here;'—both birds and bird-catchers have come thither: it is these he instructs;—'the Purāṇa is the Veda: this it is;' thus saying, let him tell some Purāṇa.
>
> (XIII, 4.3.13)

Tārkṣya was an ancient mythological personification of the sun in the form of a horse or bird and the name was later given to Garuḍa, enemy of serpents.[27] The priests related a story from the Purāṇas, a collection of stories from ancient times.

The Tenth Day :

> 'King Dharma Indra,' he says; 'his people are the Gods, and they are staying here;'—learned srotriyas (theologians) accepting no gifts, have come thither; it is these he instructs; 'the Sāman (chant-texts) are the Veda; this it is;' thus saying, let him repeat a decade of the Sāman.
>
> (XIII, 4.3.14)

Since King Dharma Indra's people were the gods, it is not surprising to find as their representatives the theologians, or possibly young theologians.[28] The day was probably set aside for theological disputes, and since it concluded one round of the legendary cycle, it was concluded with the chanting of hymns.

The Brāhmaṇa clearly expressed what was to be gained:

> In telling this revolving legend, he tells all royalties, all regions, all Vedas, all gods, all beings; and, verily, for whomsoever knows this, attains to fellowship over all people, secures for himself all the Vedas and, by gratifying the gods, finally establishes himself on all beings. This very same,

legend revolves again and again for a year; for thirty-six ten-day periods he tells it.

(XIII, 4.3.15)

The Return of the Horse and The Subsequent Ritual

When twelve moons had passed the horse returned. Recall the first injunction of the priests when the horse and its retinue were departing: NO BATHING! Therefore, the first action was to cleanse the horse. He was yoked to a golden chariot and taken to a watering place where he was bathed and garlanded by the queen and the *rājā's* lesser wives and thus made ready for his triumphant re-entry to the sacred grounds.

Crowding into the grounds came the *rājā*, now a Mahārājā, with over 400 personal attendants. His fourth wife came with 100 daughters of chamberlains and charioteers; his discarded wife was attended by 100 daughters of heralds and headmen; his favourite wife was attended by 100 noble women; his Queen was attended by 100 daughters of kings. The Mahārājā's Brahmin, now truly the Purohita, came with his retinue, the conclave of officiating priests, the teachers of the Pāriplava legend, and the minstrels. When we add to this the 400 men who had originally accompanied the horse, a very conservative estimate would be that over 2,000 officials crowded into the grounds.

Added to this scene must be the animals which were assembled about the twenty-one stakes erected under the supervision of the Adhvaryu. "About fifteen victims (animals) are bound to each of these stakes, all domestic animals, the total number being 327. In the spaces between the stakes 282 wild animals, from the elephant and the rhinoceros to the bee and the fly, are temporarily confined, to be freed when the ceremony is concluded, bringing the total number of assembled animals to 609."[29]

The horse entered the sacred ground accompanied by priests and was joined by the four wives of the Mahārājā and a young maiden as the fifth (XIII, 5.2.1). The procession ended at the sacrificial post where the horse was tied whilst the women circumambulated the post. The horse was "quieted."

Although the Mahārājā and his court remained on the ground, only the women and the priests who formed the group around the dead horse were swept along by the ritual. At the moment that the horse died, the grandeur, the pageantry, the poetry ceased.

Remember the second injunction of the priests: NO MARES! Now "the curious, almost incredible archaic rite begins of a queen's marriage to a dead beast, symbolic of the ever-living god Varuṇa, master of the order of the world."[30]

Occasionally a laconic detail, inserted by a non-committal scribe who is merely recording it as it was, brings immediacy to an ancient record, in which all participants—the low and the mighty—have long been dead, and whose joys and sufferings seem now to be only academic. For the scribe wrote that the "king's wives AND ONE MAIDEN AS A FIFTH" (XIII, 5.2.1) attend the slaughter of the horse. Later, only the wives will take needle and thread to the horse's hide. Why amongst all this plethora of detail, when thousands of attendants are present, should this one maiden be singled out for mention? I believe that this maiden was the stand-in for the Queen during the mating with the horse, which would continue throughout the night. The maiden would be too sacred or too scarred for a return to ordinary living. The *dakṣiṇā* for priests could include a maiden (XIII, 5.4.27); what more natural than that the girl who had participated in the central rite should become the property of the priest responsible for the rite of fertility?

> She lies down beside the dead horse and the Adhvaryu covers the two with a cloth. He prays: 'In heaven be ye covered, both. And may the manfully potent stallion, seed bestower, bestow the seed within.' The queen [or, as I suppose, the maiden] is to grasp and draw forth the sexual organ of the stallion, pressing it to her own.
>
> 'O Mother Mother Mother!' she cries out. 'Nobody will take me! The poor nag sleeps! Me, this wonderful little thing all dressed in the leaves and bark of the *kampila* tree!'

> The priest: 'I shall incite the procreator. Do thou, too, incite the procreator'.
>
> Whereat the queen says to the stallion: 'Come, let the two of us stretch out our limbs.'
>
> The priest prays to incite the god: 'Come, lay thy seed well in the channel of the one who has opened to thee her thighs. O thou, potent of manhood, set in motion the organ that is to women the nourisher of life. It darts into the sheath, their hidden lover, darkly buffeting, back and forth.'
>
> The queen: 'O Mother Mother Mother ! No one is taking me!'[31]

A dialogue of obscenities followed[32] and the priests commented upon it by saying "that life and the deities depart from those who at the sacrifice speak impure speech." (XIII, 2.9.9). That is, in order to retain the efficacy of the sexual rite, the priests surrounded it by a wall of non-ritual, of non-intelligence, making the potency of the spoken word impotent and laying the curse for such impurities of speech upon the women who for some reason (or un-reason) would not be affected by it.

The wives, using 101 needles of gold, silver, and copper, then marked out the lines on the horse's body for the dissector's knife to follow: these were the knife cuts which formed a path for the sacrificer's attainment of immortality.

> After butchering the horse, they caused the queen of high intelligence who was endowed with sacred knowledge, also property, and equally devotion: which are the prime qualities of a queen—to sit beside the cut up beast, while the Brahmins, cool and composed in mind, taking the marrow, duly cooked it. Whereupon the king, still following scriptures, sniffed the steam of that marrow so cooked, which is potent to purge sin. The remaining limbs of the beast were then cast into the fire by the sixteen learned priests, and the Horse Sacrifice of that World Monarch was complete.[33]

The purpose of the Aśvamedha was straightforward: the Mahārājā had demonstrated his strength and that of his kingdom —if the ceremony was completed, the completion proved his point and was at the same time, a celebration of that same superiority.

But whilst that one sacrificer was proving his temporal power the priests, by means of the Pāriplava legend, presented to the community: 36 hymns from the Ṛgveda with appropriate teachings; 36 hymns from the Sāmaveda; 36 extracts from the Yajurveda and 36 from the Atharvaveda; 36 myths of Time, creation, and destruction; 36 legends of Yama and the Fathers; 36 sacred dramas; 36 formulae of poisons or healing; 36 teachings on Demonology; 36 magic tricks; 36 extracts from the Itihāsa; 36 stories from the Purāṇas; 36 days of theological dispute. Simultaneously, the minstrels were singing their ballads of history and heroes. Therefore, the priests and the poets made of the Aśvamedha a celebration of an entire cultural heritage.

CHAPTER III

References and Notes

1. C. G. Jung, *Memories, Dreams, and Reflections* recorded and edited by A. Jaffe, Glossary, "collective unconscious."

2. Ibid; Glossary, "archetype."

3. For example : the use of cavalry at Royal Processions in London, or at the burial of John F. Kennedy in the U.S A.

4. Sir Edwin Arnold, *The Light of Asia*, p. 70.

5. Compare the conversion of Saul/Paul to Christianity. Although no horse was mentioned in Acts 9.3, the 18th century Italian artist, Caravaggion depicted Saul/Paul as mounted at the beginning of his experience. Jung : *Man and his Symbols*, p. 46, illustration.

6. Jung : ed. *Man and his Symbols*, p. 174.

7. Dutt : *A History of Civilisation in Ancient India* I, p. 143 and also R. Dutt, *Mahabharata, the Epic of Ancient India.*

8. Dowson, *A Classical Dictionary of Hindu Mythology*, "manu."

9. Ibid : "Sūrya."

10. Ibid : "Genealogy of the Surya-Vansa," p. 313.

11. Ibid : "Genealogy of the Chandra-Vansa," pp. 69, 70.

12. *Manvantara*: "In the time of Alexander the Great the Hindus did not claim a greater antiquity than 6777 A.C. The mode of reckoning . . . for yugas. . . is very simple. Given the precession of 49.8 seconds as determined by Hipparchus, the period of one revolution through the whole circle of 360 degrees would be 26,024,16/166 years. Getting rid of the fraction in the usual way by multiplying by 166 and adding 16=4,320,000." K. S. Mac Donald, *Sacred Books of the East, Examined and Described*: British Museum Extract. Similarly, Dowson : *A Classical Dictionary of Hindu Mythology*, "manvantara" where the period is of 4,320,000 years.

13. With regard to note 12, compare H. Zimmer, *Myths and Symbols in Indian Art and Civilization*, ed. Joseph Campbell (Bollingen Series VI), pp. 17, 18, where a Mahāyuga is 4,320,000 and a kalpa 1,000 times a mahāyuga. Every kalpa is divided into 14 manvantaras which makes the duration of a Manvantara 3067200000 years and therefore the years preceding the birth of the present manu would be approximately 18403200000 years.

14. Dowson : *A Classical Dictionary of Hindu Mythology*, "Janaka."

15, 16, 17. Ibid : "Nimi."

18. Ibid : "Gandharvas."

19. Naama Drury : *The Vedic Rishi*, pp. 6, 7.

20. Dowson : *A Classical Dictionary of Hindu Mythology*, "Gandharva-Veda."

21. *New Larousse Encyclopedia of Mythology*, p. 343.

22. Dowson : *A Classical Dictionary of Hindu Mythology*, "Kuvera."

23. Ibid : "Raksasas."

24. S. Cammann : "Islamic and Indian Magic Squares," Parts I & II, *History of Religions, An International Journal for Comparative Historical Studies*, ed. M. Eliade, J. Kitagawa, C. Long. Vol. VIII (1969-1970) Nos. 2 & 4, pp. 181, 271.

25. Eggeling, Part V, p. 368, fn. 3.

26. As, for instance, the humiliation of kissing the Sow of Gretz. James A. Michener, *The Source*, p. 770.

27. Dowson : *A Classical Dictionary of Hindu Mythology*, "Tarkshya."

28. Eggeling, Part V, p. 370, fn. 2.

29. Griffith, Yajurveda, p. 258.

30. Campbell, *Oriental Mythology*, p. 194.

31. Ibid : p. 195.

32. *The dialogue between the Queen and the priest.* Griffith did not translate the relevant passage in the Yajurveda (XXIII, 19 to 31) because "this (the second half of verse 19 and the following 9 verses) are not reproducible even in the semi obscurity of a learned European language and stanzas 30, 31 would be unintelligible without them." The dialogue may be found in Campbell, *Oriental Mythology*, pp. 195, 196, citing J. J. Meyer, Trilogie altindischer Machte und Feste der Vegetation (Zurich and Leipzig: Mac Nichans Verlag, 1937) Part III, pp. 241-46.

33. Campbell, *Oriental Mythology*, p. 197, citing Mahābhārata 14.89.2-6.

CHAPTER IV

THE AGNICAYANA I

The Prajāpati Creation Myth

Why trends or ideas of a cultural, political, artistic, or religious significance were manifested simultaneously by societies having little or no apparent communication with each other has puzzled scholars since Frazer's comparative material made cross-cultural studies stimulating, provocative,[1] and (as time would show) too simplistic.

Thinkers and innovators in ancient civilizations were concerned with the question: "How did the created world come into existence?", not as an academic or scientific enquiry but as an emotional and religious need. The most sophisticated answers to the question came from cultures situated between the Eastern Mediterranean and the Ganges River. In myths other than Indian, I will refer especially to the myths of the Ancient Egyptians,[2] the Hebrew legend in Genesis,[3] and the Babylonian creation epic "Enuma Elish."[4] Travellers entering India may have brought with them their creation legends or the *brāhmaṇas* may have travelled abroad, but it is unlikely that influences from the outside accounted for any significant amount of the Brahmanic material, because inherited myths in all ancient societies were the property of the priesthood who guarded their knowledge jealously. Within their own cultural inheritance, looking back over the Vedic hymns and mythology, some of which formed the material for the Pāriplava legend—the *brāhmaṇas* would not have found a rich source of material for answering questions pertaining to creation. The renewal of the world after the flood and Indra's slaying of Vṛtra were important myths, but not creation myths in the true sense of the word.

The periodic creation and destruction of the world and the *manvantaras* were concepts rather than myths. There was a god called Viśvakarman who was "all deeds" in a practical sense, a creative craftsman who built palaces for the gods. Bose commented :

> If a question lies beyond the powers of knowledge the Jñānayogin will rather leave it unanswered. For example, in answer to the question whether the uncreated universe was upheld by the Creator, the Ṛgvedic sage gives a bold answer:
>
> > He who surveys it in the highest region, He truly, knows it, or maybe, He does not know! (R.V., X.129.7).[5]

Nevertheless, the *ṛṣis* did not quite leave the question alone for, although the hymn quoted by Bose does finish with a question mark, in the earlier stanzas of the same hymn some speculation (though not dogmatic) has been made on the origins of creation.

> There was not the non-existent nor the existent then . . . X.129.1
> That one (tad ekam) breathed, windless, by its own power . . . X.129.2
> That which, coming into being, was covered with the void that One arose through the power of heat . . . X.129.3.[6]

Therefore, according to this hymn, creation begins with the emergence of Tad Ekam from the realms of the non-existent and the existent, and ends with the *ṛṣis'* questioning the extent of the deities' omniscience since they, like man, come after the beginnings of creation.

The *Puruṣa sūkta* (R.V., X.90) presents two themes of origin: one of emanation, and one of sacrifice, and the themes are developed side by side. Puruṣa is partly manifest in creation, whilst the remainder of Puruṣa is outside of creation:

> Three-fourths of Puruṣa ascended,
> the fourth part was here again and again,
> and, diversified in form, it moved
> to the animate and the inanimate world.
>
> (R.V., X.90.4)

In order to create the world, Puruṣa had been sacrificed by the *devas* (X.90.6) thus "the Deity allowed his absoluteness to be sacrificed so that he could be manifested in the world of space and time."[7] It follows that, should he withdraw his support of creation by withdrawing his essence into himself, then creation would disintegrate and lose its manifest form. According to the Vedas, the highest virtue is to sacrifice oneself for a noble cause (for example, the sacrifice of Yama in R.V. X. 13.4), therefore, the "Deity is the Prototype of the virtuous man; he sacrifices himself for the glory of creation."[8]

In "writing" the Prajāpati myth, the *brāhmaṇas* accepted the themes of creation by emanation and creation by sacrifice, but the themes were now centred on Prajāpati, not Puruṣa, and Prajāpati's role as the demi-urge became clearly defined.

The Sanskrit word for creation is *sṛṣṭi* ($\sqrt{}$*sṛj*=emission); Campbell translated *sṛṣṭi* as "what is poured forth."[9] Here, then, is the Creation or the Pouring Forth of the Universe, according to the *brāhmaṇas* of the Agnicayana rite.

The Prajāpati Creation Myth

> Verily, in the beginning, there was here the Non-existent; the Non-existent was the *ṛṣis* (vital airs; toil and austerity) and the *ṛṣis* were the Non-existent. (VI, 1.1.1)
>
> [The *ṛṣis* were the vital airs, and the vital airs were the Non-existent, therefore the Non-existent was the *ṛṣis*, and the vital airs.]
>
> In the midst of the vital airs was Indra who kindled the vital airs by the power (*indriya*) and since Indra kindled (*indh*) therefore he is the kindler (*indha*). The kindler they called Indra, mystically. (VI, 1. 1. 2)

The Gods Love the Mystic.

> Now within the Non-existent, each part the equal of the others and of the whole, existed or non-existed the *ṛṣis*, the vital airs, Indra the power, and Indha the kindler. And Indra kindled the vital airs. When kindled the vital airs created seven separate *puruṣas* or personalities, (VI, 1.1.2) [souls, or entities] but these seven *puruṣas* could not generate and therefore the seven combined into one person. Two

puruṣas formed the area above the navel, one of them the area below the navel, one *puruṣa* was a wing or arm, one *puruṣa* was the other wing or arm, and one *puruṣa* was the base, feet, or tail. The life sap, *rasa*, of the seven combined to become the head, and therefore in the head they concentrated the excellence śrī. (VI, 1.1.4)

This One Person is Prajāpati, the Lord of Generation. (VI, 1.1.5)

Prajāpati desired to be reproduced and having practised austerity, he poured forth the Brahman, [which is also prayer and the sacred syllable Aum] and the triple science of the Veda. [Within the Brahman was Vāc, the language of men and animals, voice and sound, and Vāc was feminine.] (VI, 1.1.8)

Therefore Prajāpati created the waters out of Vāc. Water pervaded everything; water covered everything. (VI, 1.1.9)

Prajāpati with the triple science entered the waters and formed an egg. (VI, 1.1.10) Prajāpati touched it and said "let it exist" and from it the Brahman and the triple science were born." (VI, 1.1.10) Brahman is first born of all even before Prajāpati. (VI, 1.1.10)

The egg from which the Brahman was born had as its embryo the foremost (agri) mystically Agni. (VI, 1.1.11)

The Gods Love the Mystic

As the embryonic liquid emerged it became aśva, the horse, as that which cried (ras) the rāsabha (the ass). The juice adhering to the shell of the egg became the he-goat and the shell became the earth. (VI, 1.1.11)

Prajāpati desired to generate earth from waters. He threw the shell into the water. The juice became a tortoise, that which spirted upwards, what is over the water. The whole earth dissolved over the waters; all the universe is one form of water (VI, 1.1.12.) Prajāpati toiled and formed clay, and saline soil, sand, gravel, rock, ore, gold, plants, trees, therewith he clothed the earth. (VI, 1.1.13)

The earth became foundation bhū = bhūmi = earth, the becoming or arising one, and Prajāpati spread it out (prath) therefore the broad one, Pṛthivī. (VI, 1.1.15)

The earth thought herself beautiful and sang (gā) therefore the earth is Gāyatrī. (VI, 1.1.15)

Prajāpati then assumed the form of Agni, impregnated the earth and produced an egg of which:

1. The embryo was wind (Vāyu).
2. The tear was the birds.
3. The juice was sun-motes.
4. The shell was the air. (VI, 1.2.2)

Prajāpati by means of Vāyu and air made an egg of which:

1. The embryo was the sun.
2. The tear was variegated pebbles.
3. The juice was sunbeams.
4. The shell was the sky. (VI, 1.2.3)

Prajāpati by means of the sun and the sky made an egg of which:

1. The embryo was the moon.
2. The tear was the stars.
3. The juice was the intermediate quarters.
4. The shell was the points of the compass. (VI, 1.2.4)

Having created these worlds Prajāpati desired to create the creatures, but creatures were special, not to be derived from an egg, but from Prajāpati's mind with the assistance of Vāc. (VI, 1.2.6)

Therefore, Prajāpati's mind with Vāc produced eight drops, the eight Vasus, the bright, good, and beneficent, and these were all placed on earth (VI, 1.2.6). Then Prajāpati's mind with Vāc produced eleven drops, the Rudras, and these were all placed in the air. (VI, 1.2.7)

Then Prajāpati's mind together with Vāc produced twelve drops, the twelve Ādityas, creatures of infinity, and these he placed in the sky. (VI, 1.2.8)

Then Prajāpati's mind together with Vāc produced the All-gods and these were placed in the quarters. (VI, 1.2.9)

By this time the fruits of the earth had ripened and Prajāpati ate of them and became pregnant within himself. When the time was auspicious, he emitted from the upper vital airs—the gods, and from the lower vital airs—mortals. (VI, 1.2.11)

Then Prajāpati relaxed and the vital airs went out of him and the gods left him. (VI, 1.2.12)

Bases of Interpretation

The Circular Form

The myth is easier to understand if it is first thought of as emanating in circle upon circle. The cosmic centre could be named the Existent, but was otherwise incomprehensible to man's intellect and his intuitive faculties, and therefore the *brāhmaṇas* commenced with the Non-existent, since creation necessarily begins with either the Non-existent or chaotic matter. The *brāhmaṇas* were thus continuing the principle, already expressed in the Ṛgveda, that there is an Existent beyond our human apprehension that exists or non-exists beyond the "not-yet-existent." Gods and creation emerge from the not-yet-existent.

In terms of the myth, the Non-existent had within itself, latent and undifferentiated, the *ṛṣis*, the vital airs, Indra, and Indha. The myth emphasizes the identification of the whole Non-existent with the parts and the parts with the whole, and the parts with each other. The parts may be thought of as whirling out of the Non-existent, forming patterns, receding. Emphasis is on co-identity, co-existence, mutual dependence.

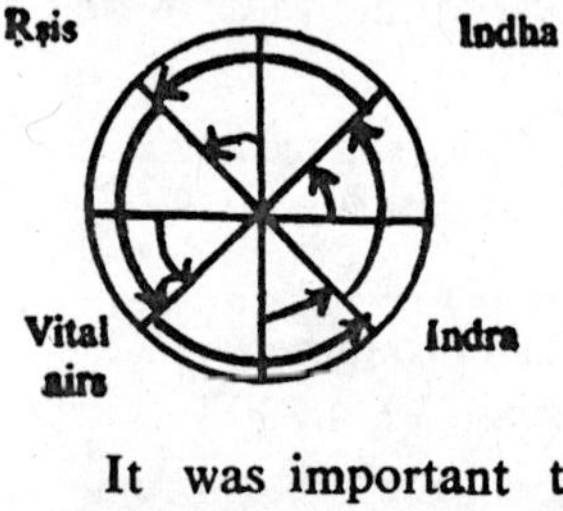

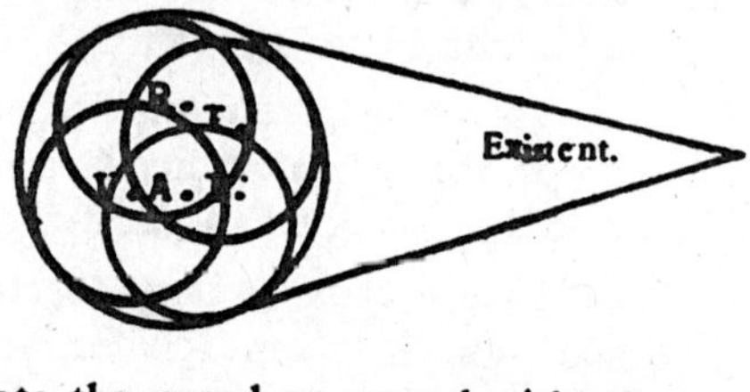

It was important to associate the word or sound with the object being brought into existence. Cultures as basically different as Ancient Egyptian and Australian Aborigine have recognized "name" as the essence o f self or personality. Here the *brāhmaṇas* have placed Indra into the Non-existent as a force or power. To be powerful and forceful was always Indra's role, but here the god who had been first amongst the gods (above pp. 34-35) has been de-personalized.

Within the Non-existent the vital airs created seven *puruṣas* which formed into one body, Prajāpati. It may be seen from the following diagram that the figure is either human, angelic, or birdlike, according to the placement and style of the limbs.

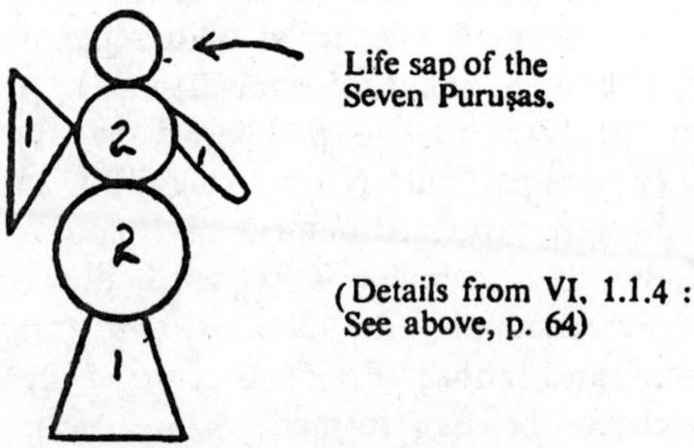

Creation legends must take one tremendous leap from the Non-existent to the universally existent at the point of the demi-urge, and now this myth follows that pattern, but, again, in a circular form. *Prajāpati poured forth Brahman*, the sacred syllable Aum and the three Vedas; within Brahman was Vāc, the language of man and animals, voice and sound. Out of Vāc Prajāpati created the waters (the moisture pervading animal and plant life as well as ocean, etc.). Prajāpati, the three Vedas and Brahman entered the waters and formed an egg. Prajāpati by touch and sound, let it exist, and from the egg the Brahman and the triple science were born. But *Brahman is first born of all even before Prajāpati.* The circle is again complete.

Because an egg could fully develop new life within its shell, it became a symbol in the ancient world for completeness, renewal, and immortality. The old saying "which came first, the chicken or the egg ?" demonstrates what a natural choice the egg is for the self-contained circle-motif, by which will be created the sun, moon, stars, air, wind, and birds. Only supernatural creatures, the gods, and men were directly created by Prajāpati—creatures by Prajāpati's mind and the spoken word, gods and men by Prajāpati's self-impregnation.

The Linear Form

As well as emanating in circle upon circle the myth can be expressed progressively by numerals, especially numbers based on four or the square. The *brāhmaṇas* were obsessed by numbers,[10] especially as a means of reducing phenomena to a simple basis; the months of the year can obviously be numbered from as simple a method as marking the position of the rising sun, but the *brāhmaṇas* also attempted to give parts of the human body a numerical equivalent. (IX,1.1.43) It is obvious from the texts that they knew division and multiplication, and they were particularly impressed by 3, and 3 times 3.

If the myth were expressed numerically (pattern in notes)[11] it would be found that a whole was frequently divided into four components. For example, the Non-existent formed the *ṛṣis*, vital airs, Indra, and Indha; Prajāpati formed Brāhman and the triple science; the Egg formed Agni, Aśva, Aga, and Earth; the Egg formed Wind, Birds, Sun-motes, and Air; the Egg formed Moon, Stars, Intermediate Quarters, Points of the Compass. Four is symbolically perfect in the sense of being a perfectly harmonious pattern. The use of four and the quarternary can be correlated from many cultures, the most obvious usage being as patterns for cities (heavenly and earthly) and for temples.[12]

The numeral, seven, used only once in the myth when the seven *puruṣas* formed Prajāpati, is symbolic of a perfect period or cycle, comprises the union of ternary and quarternary, and is the number basic to many groups, for example, musical notes.[13] When Prajāpati's mind combined with Vāc, the *eight* Vasus, the *twelve* Ādityas, and the all-gods in the four quarters were created. The aptness of the choice of numbers can be judged by the fact that eight is related to the intermediate form between the terrestrial order and the circle (the eternal order)[14] and that the eight Vasus were the personifications of natural phenomena between earth and heaven, for example, the pole star or dawn.[15] Twelve is the number of the Zodiac, linked with notions of time and space, and the wheel or circle. The twelve[16] Ādityas (actually there were not always twelve)[17] were manifestations of the sun, months of the year, and creatures of infinity. The all-gods in the four quarters (Viśvadevas) were probably expressive of divinity, multiplicity, and infinity in creation.

The point being made is not just that this underlying numerical pattern existed, but that the numbers selected can be shown to be archetypal imagery whose meaning remains true on a cross-cultural basis.

The Death of God Theme

The Prajāpati myth is a myth of many themes (creation out of nothing, creation by word, creation by god's self-impregnation) and of many motifs (numbers, fruit, eggs) and these themes were not unique to it. (I have to qualify this statement by saying that, to my knowledge, this is the only myth in which the earth sings.) However, apart from the earth singing, each theme or motif had appeared in other creation legends, so that it was not in the types of themes used that the Prajāpati myth was different—but in the fact that it combined so many of them, and used each one so profusely. When creation was completed Prajāpati relaxed, the vital airs went out of him, and the gods left him. This is the "death of god" theme, and the creation legends known to us have ended with, or led into, this theme—Utnapishtim's gods withdrew to the heavens; the Egyptian Osiris was dismembered. The theme is of continuing importance to the human race for it seems that mankind retains some traumatic memory of a time when the gods deserted the human race. It is not only a collective experience, but can be experienced individually as, for example, in Nietzsche's famous passage.[18]

Co-incident with the death of god is the end of the Golden Age; Adam and Eve were expelled from the Garden of Eden, Seth's rule brought anarchy to Egypt, Utnapishtim's world was destroyed by flood. Each culture then takes up those elements of creation and fall which were peculiar to it and forms a new myth of the restoration of god and the salvation of man. Utnapishtim offered sacrifice in order to tempt the gods out of heaven. Osiris' body having been dissected and scattered to the four quarters—his wife Isis seeks out all parts of his body, puts them together, impregnates herself and gives birth to a son, Horus, who re-establishes the reign of his father. The Hebrew myth waited many centuries for the Christian conclusion in which Mary, miraculously impregnated by the spirit of god, gives birth to a son who reconciles god and man and re-establishes the reign of his father. Thus, in both Egyptian and Christian, salvation was through the birth of the son of god and the *brāhmaṇas* concluded their myth in a thematically similar way.

The Prajāpati Creation Myth: Restoration

Salvation came through the creative principle of a female, Uṣas, who was impregnated by Prajāpati in an unnatural way, for their relationship (daughter/father) was incestuous and criticized as sinful by the *brāhmaṇas*.

Uṣas gave birth to a son, Kumāra. Because Kumāra cried Prajāpati asked of him, "My boy, why do you cry?" and the boy answered, "I have no name given me; give me a name." Because he cried Prajāpati named him Rudra.

But the boy was ambitious and replied: "Surely I am mightier than that; give me yet a name." Prajāpati continued to give him names, but each time the boy was dissatisfied and continued to ask for more.

These names were bestowed on Kumāra:
Thou art Rudra.
Thou art Sarva, for Sarva is the waters.
Thou art Paśupati, for Paśupati is the plants.
Thou art Ugra, for Ugra is Vāyu, the wind.
Thou art Aśani, for Aśani is the lightning.
Thou art Bhava, for Bhava is Parjanya, the rain-god.
Thou art Mahān Devah, for the moon is Prajāpati, and Prajāpati is the Great God.
Thou art Īśāṇa, for Īśāṇa is the sun which rules over all.
Prajāpati had bestowed his powers on his son.

(Precis: VI, 1.3.8. to 17).

The *brāhmaṇas* also made a theological statement of the same theme. When Prajāpati realized that his strength had gone, he asked Agni to restore him and Agni did so. Now whichever of the sons succeeds, the father, grandfather, son, and grandsons are called after him (VI, 1.2.13), therefore, Prajāpati is called after Agni. The father, Prajāpati, is also the son. Prajāpati created Agni, therefore he is Agni's father; Agni restored Prajāpati, and is therefore Prajāpati's father.

Egyptian, Christian, or Brahmanic, the point is made. The

son who re-establishes communication between god and man is also the father, BUT, in order that the new-formed channels of communication may remain open, forever reassuring man of his salvation, man must perpetuate in ritual the climax of the restoration. As that ritual action, the *brāhmaṇas* built the fire altar. They then added a new dimension. Creation had so weakened the godhead that the *brāhmaṇas* were needed to restore his vigour by means of the ritual, and—by a process of identification—when a *brāhmaṇa* thus restored god, he built his own niche in eternity.

CHAPTER IV

References and Notes

1. Many of the anthropologists of the early twentieth century admit that their interest in the subject was fired by Frazer's comparative material. B. Malinowski, for instance.

2. J. Caster, *Wings of the Falcon*, Section II, p. 6.

3. Genesis 1.1-31.

4. Mircea Eliade, *From Primitive to Zen.*

5. Bose : *Hymns from the Vedas*, p. 56.

6. Macdonell : *A Vedic Reader for Students*, p. 207.

7. Bose : *Hymns from the Vedas*, fn. to St. 6, p. 287.

8. Ibid : fn. to St. 16, p. 289.

9. Campbell, *Oriental Mythology*, p. 10.

10. For example, IX, 1.2.16 where a count is made from 10 to 100,000 millions to a billion. In France, U.S.A. a "billion"=1,000 millions; in England, a million millions.

11. *Numerical pattern of the Prajāpati myth*:—

The Existent

Non-Existent — Zero

ṛṣis | vital airs | Indra | Indha — 4

---

7 Puruṣas — 7

Prajāpati — 1

Prajāpati — 1

Brāhman | Triple Science — 4

Prajāpati and Vāc — 2

waters — 1

Prajāpati | triple science | Brāhman | waters — 6

Egg — 1

Agni | Aśva | Aga | Earth — 4

Foot-note 11 Contd.

Prajāpati/Agni and Earth	2
Egg	1
Wind — Birds — Sun-motes — Air	4
Prajāpati/Vāyu and Air	2
Egg	1
Moon — Stars — Inter. Qrtrs. — Compass Pts.	4
Prajāpati's mind and Vāc	2
8 Vasus	8
Prajāpati's mind and Vāc	2
11 Rudras	11
Prajāpati's mind and Vāc	2
12 Ādityas	12
Prajāpati's mind and Vāc	2
All-gods in four quarters	multiplicity
Prajāpati	1
gods — mortals.	2

12. J. E. Cirlot, *A Dictionary of Symbols*, trans. Jack Sage. "Four"; "Quarternary."

13. Ibid : "Seven."

14. Ibid : "Eight."

15. Dowson : *A Classical Dictionary of Hindu Mythology*, "Vasu." The eight were : water, pole star, moon, earth, wind, fire, dawn, light.

16. Cirlot : *Symbols*, "Twelve."

17. Dowson : *A Classical Dictionary of Hindu Mythology*, "Aditya."

18. Nietzsche, *Thus Spoke Zarathustra*, trans. R. J. Hollingdale, Intro. p. xiv.

CHAPTER V

THE AGNICAYANA II

The Ritual

A succession of ritual geniuses had fashioned the Aśvamedha into the epitome of regal celebrations for the *kṣatriya*, half of that ever on-going dichotomy—*kṣatriya* and *brāhmaṇa*, Emperor and Pope, Henry and Beckett, State and Church. By contrast, in the Agnicayana—a priest's ritual for priests, we find that the heroic, the lustiness, the fertility emphases of the Aśvamedha, have no place. The text implies (by specifying the number of kindling sticks to be used by a *kṣatriya*) that either a *brāhmaṇa* or a *kṣatriya* might be the sacrificer. However, when a *brāhmaṇa* performed the service for a *kṣatriya*, the *brāhmaṇa* by that action surrendered his own hope of immortality. (IX, 5.2.13)

A Personal Tradition

It was probably because it was such an exclusive, individual rite, that the Agnicayana became sealed within the priesthood by a personal tradition. "For even as people hand on from one to the other a full vessel, in the same way they (the priests) hand down that sacrifice from one to the other." (I, 5.2.7). In the Yajurveda the personal seal of the Agnicayana was that of Aṅgiras, and that Veda has a repeated refrain, "in Aṅgiras manner" or "as Aṅgiras was wont to do." Aṅgiras was reputed to have composed some hymns of the Ṛgveda; he was one of the seven *maharṣis*. As a human, he was a writer on astronomy; as an astronomical personification, he was Bṛhaspati, the regent of the planet Jupiter.[1]

By the time of the Śatapatha Brāhmaṇa, Aṅgiras had been replaced by a line of teachers, each of whom passed the teaching to his successor.[2] Knowledge of ritual was then said to have originated from Prajāpati who was *the* progenitor of mankind rather than from Aṅgiras, *one* of the ten progenitors of mankind. Whilst the authority of the Yajurveda had been "as Aṅgiras was wont to do," the Brāhmaṇa authorized its actions by "so Śāṇḍilya was wont to say," thus Aṅgiras *does* but Śāṇḍilya *says*. Between Aṅgiras and Śāṇḍilya was a line of *brāhmaṇas*-teachers-innovators who revitalized their part of the ritual, not by returning to past Vedic glories, not by altering the ritual actions, but by interpreting these actions so that their new interpretation gave a different meaning to them. To the man who had performed the Agnicayana the Yajurveda promised material prosperity in his lifetime and a personal commendation to the gods at his death; the Śatapatha Brāhmaṇa promised immortality. As we have seen, the *brāhmaṇas* achieved this new emphasis by claiming that the ritual actions materialized the creation-salvation myth of Prajāpati.

The need to build a fire altar came to a man when he had reached the time of life when some positive action seemed necessary to prolong, in some other form of existence, a life which had become too precious to end at the death of its present body. In the antiquity in which the Agnicayana was ritually developed life after death was an undefined existence with Yama and the Pitṛs. The Agnicayana was a very positive ceremony; it expressed a belief in an afterlife as tangible as the Ancient Egyptian belief which perpetuated itself in stone. It was a ritual for the individual; one man ventured out to find his own immortality.

Preparatory Rites

Preparation was important and, because of the articles to be used, expensive. As always, the locality was carefully chosen. It must be fairly extensive since the altar itself would cover over 300 square feet and additional areas were needed for accompanying fires, for temporary shelters, for sacrificial stakes, and for a pit dedicated to Nirṛti, to whom all things out-caste from the ceremony as ritually redundant or negatively charged were consigned. Water must be nearby for the practical purpose of brick-making and for use in ritual cleansing and purification, and so that the ashes of the sacred fire may be returned daily to the water from which Agni (fire) has been born. Most important of all—the sacred area required an unobstructed view eastward because the earthly fire was identified with its counterpart, the sun, which as Savitṛ was honoured with the first words of the Yajurveda text:

> Harnessing, first of all the mind, Savitar having stretched the thought.
> With reverent look upon the light of Agni bore them up from earth.
> By impulse of God Savitar, with our spirit harnessed strive with might of win the heavenly.
> Savitar, having harnessed Gods who go to light and heavenly thought,
> Who will create the lofty light—Savitar urge them on their way.
>
> (Y.V. XI, 1.2 and 3)

The sacrificer had completed a period of preparation and abstained from certain foods and sexual intercourse. His wife shared these personal prohibitions and assisted in the ritual, but there is no indication that she shared its benefits. The rite of satī, in which a widow burned herself on the funeral pyre of her husband thereby attaining immortality for his soul—could be a distorted form of the Agnicayana.

The *brāhmaṇas* described the initiation as an oath to the sacrifice, a dedication to complete the ritual once begun. In a sense, the entire sacrifice was an initiation and a dedication—from being one's mortal self to recognising the eternal, immortal self. The sacrifice stood at the mouth of the sacrifice ready to pass from the external and profane to the inward and sacred. A thousand mile journey must begin with the first step, a step from the security of the familiar into the insecurity of the alien. A man does not venture without knowledge or an experienced guide. Because this initial step was dangerous and its successful undertaking vital to success, the sacrificer chose a time when circumstances appeared at their most auspicious—not only at the beginning of his solar year, but on the day of the new moon of that special year.[8]

It happened that Sinīvālī "with fair braids with beauteous crest with lovely locks" (Y.V. XI, 56) was the goddess of the first day of the new moon. She was also the goddess of childbirth and with her help the new immortal self of the sacrificer will be born. Especially was she the sacrificer's anima figure,[4] the priestess-goddess who held the secret of entry, his first guide into out-of-this-world regions.

The Sacrifice

Probably because the culmination of the ritual was meant to be sunny, light-orientated, and immortality-granting, the slaughter of the victims took place when the moon, the antithesis of positive light, that queen of ancient rites, of instinctual drives never intellectually expressed, was supreme in her night kingdom. At the full moon of Phālguna, when in the ghostly moonlight, half-seen images are fully seen as something else, the sacrificer paid in full his price of entry to the ritual proper. On sacrificial stakes placed in line from north to south so that the rising sun caught in its first rays the rigid bodies, grotesquely headless, were five sacrificial victims:—one he-goat, one bull, one ram, one horse, and one man. The purpose was "to slaughter them for different deities:—the Puruṣa (man) for Viśvakarman, the horse for Varuṇa, the bull for Indra, the ram for Tvashtri, the he-goat for Agni." (VI, 2.1.5) Although the Solar Zodiac and its symbols did not come into India from Greece until after the time of the Śatapatha Brāhmaṇa,[5] it is interesting to note that four of the sacrificial victims are symbols for signs of the Zodiac (goat/Capricorn; bull/Taurus; ram/Aries; man/Aquarius). Further, a pair of horses, one black and one white, have represented the twins, Gemini.[6] A white horse was used to protect the altar site after sunset.

The bodies of these victims were placed in the water intended for brick-making and the heads, perhaps impaled on stakes as a warning to trespassers of the significant ritual being conducted, were kept for ritual purposes.

Now that so many components were grouping together to form the desired pattern, the priest prayed:

> I yoke with prayer your ancient inspiration; may the laud rise as on the prince's pathway.

All Sons of the Immortal One shall hear it, who have resorted to celestial dwellings.

(Y.V. XI,5)

The Firepan

A search must be made for the clay from which a firepan will be moulded. A horse was led forward and expected to indicate by pawing with his hoof, a deposit of clay beneath the surface. (VI, 3.2.1 ff).

O courser, having come to earth, seek Agni with a longing wish
Tell us by trampling on the ground where we may dig him from the earth.

(Y.V. XI,19)

When the clay was found—or re-discovered, since it is very likely that the deposit had been placed there beforehand—the area was encircled three times in order to protect the clay from the Rākṣasas. When the clay was dug up and formally shaped, the priests invoked the assistance of Sinīvālī and the great mother-goddess, Aditi, because the pan was to give birth to the sacred fire. The pan was then made holy by incantations of magical sevens which invoked many feminine influences: those of the divine wives of the gods, those of the divine Dhiṣaṇās, those of the divine protectresses, of the divine ladies dear to the gods, of the divine ladies with unclipped wings (the lunar *nakṣatras*). (VI, 5.4.4-8) A fire was lighted in the completed pan and, for a year, taken in daily procession to water so that the ashes may be returned to the water in which Agni had been generated.

Feminine Influence

It is clear that the feminine in many forms has been dominant in these preliminaries. Although the ceremony was commenced at a conjunction of lunar and solar times, the moon has been important as a divine representation. The moon, of course, was a male god (Soma), but that was not specified here; at least the new moon was the feminine Sinīvālī. Although Savitṛ and

Agni (especially in sun form) have been formally prayed to, the goddesses Sinīvālī and Aditi, and the gods' consorts, the personalized *śaktis* or powers of their husbands, were the ones who actually assisted the ritual into being. They were aided by the influence of feminine personifications of astral and lunar significance. These positive and creative aspects of the feminine will be joined by another figure, Nirṛti, the destructive female, a shadowy figure of death, evil, and misfortune. Nirṛti is the "other" as opposed to life, goodness, health, good fortune, and all desirable aspects of human life. An altar will be built for her of black bricks baked from husks of rice, the leftover altar. The possibility of intrusion by other elements was ever-present in the Brahmanic mind: curse or bless, death or immortality; for every positive, a lurking negative. The Vedic poets had created a unique poetry from this dualism; the ritualists built a side altar to Nirṛti.

Such a predominantly feminine content testifies to the antiquity of the Agnicayana and a case could be made that the *brāhmaṇas* not only created a Prajāpati legend but also imposed a sun, masculine-orientated form on an existing moon-female-orientated rite. In fact, in II,1.2.18 ff. the *brāhmaṇas* named the *nakṣatras* which were suitable for the setting up of fires, then added a rider stating that the sun had taken their force (*na kṣatra*, not power) and that fires might therefore be set up under the sun. It is clear that the selection of an auspicious time was being changed from moon time to sun time and this implies a period of transition.

The Neck Ornament

In pursuance of the solar emphasis the sacrificer hung around his neck a circular piece of gold with twenty-one knobs on it, sewn into a black antelope skin and strung above the navel on a hempen string of three strands.

Eggeling[7] compared this plate with its 21 knobs to a passage in I, 3.4.13 where 21 verses are said to represent 12 months, 5 seasons, and 3 worlds (earth, atmosphere, sun) with the sun itself as the twenty-first, that is, the sun is represented twice.

At least two other interpretations are possible:—

1. The plate is the moon and the 21 knobs are 13 months, 5 seasons, and 3 worlds. Or

2. The plate is the sun and the 21 knobs are 13 months, 5 seasons, and 3 worlds (earth, atmosphere, moon).

According to the *brāhmaṇas* the plate is the sun and the knobs the rays of the sun (VI, 7.1.2) and it was as a symbol of the sun that it was placed around the sacrificer's neck.

Regular rites and prayers

Throughout the year some rites and prayers were repeated regularly. For example, it was customary *to raise and lower the firepan* with prayers in praise of Agni.

> High hath the Mighty risen before the Mornings, and come to us with light from out the darkness.
> Fair-shapen Agni with white-shining splendour hath filled at birth all human habitations.
>
> (Y.V.XII,13.)

> Dweller in noblest place, mid men, in truth, in sky, born of flood, kine, truth, mountain, he is holy Law, The Great.
>
> (Y.V. XII,14)

For part of each day of the year the sacrificer was to carry Agni (as fire) in order to derive full benefit from the initiation ceremony and the Agnicayana generally.[8] Directions were also given for the carrying of Agni in a chariot drawn by two oxen (VI, 8.1.8) during which time the sacrificer praised Agni as "brilliant with propitious flames" but prayed for the protection of his people from "the great shining flames." (VI, 8.1.9) When the axle of the chariot creaked, it was thought that Agni spoke. (VI, 8.1.11)

At the completion of any special offering the priests uttered a special cry, the *Vaṣaṭ call* (XIII, 1.2.3). The significance of sound rather than a word or a coherent phrase is in keeping with the belief in the efficacy of sound—always embodied in the syllable *Aum.*[9] The Vaṣaṭ call must have been very distinctive for Haug[10] observed that the priests did not dare to pronounce this sound except at the time of sacrifice for, if it were used at any other time, the priest would be cursed by the gods.

Two rites, one of prayer (the Vātsapra) and one of action (the Viṣṇu strides) were to be performed on alternate days.

The *Vātsapra* was the repetition of a Ṛgvedic hymn written by a *ṛṣi*, Vātsapri.

> First Agni sprang to life from out of heaven; the second time from us came Jātavedas.
>
> Thirdly the Manly-souled was in the waters. The pious lauds and kindles him Eternal.
>
> Agni, we know thy three powers in three stations, we know thy forms in many a place divided.
>
> We know what name supreme thou hast in secret; we know the source from which thou hast proceeded.
>
> (Y.V. XII, 18.19)
> (R.V. X. 45)

The *rite of the Viṣṇu strides* appears to be based on the only anthropomorphic traits [given to Viṣṇu in the Ṛgveda]—the strides he takes. There can be no doubt that these three steps refer to the course of the "sun, and in all probability to its passage through the three divisions of the world: earth, air, and heaven."[11]

A myth developed about the three steps of Viṣṇu, in which Viṣṇu incarnated, as the good principle, in the form of a dwarf *brāhmaṇa* to overcome Bali. When Bali asked the *brāhmaṇa* to choose a gift, the *brāhmaṇa* asked for the land he could encompass in three steps. Bali, seeing only a dwarf, readily granted such a wish, only to find himself confronted by the wide-stepping Viṣṇu.[12] The only possible association I can find between this myth and the ritual is that the sacrificial victim dedicated to Viṣṇu at the Aśvamedha was a dwarf (cow), (XIII, 2.2.9) which is a very tenuous association.

According to the Brāhmaṇa the first step was the earth, the second step the aerial expanse, and the third the sky. (I, 9.3.11) By his repetition of the Viṣṇu strides, the sacrificer attained those worlds.

The Altar

Preparation of the Site

A site was prepared and a hearth built to receive fire from the firepan and, because this fire would eventually furnish the fire for the great altar, it was shaped like a bird—for the shape of the embryo is the shape of that which is born from it. (VI, 7.2.7). In order that evil may be averted from this hearth the altar to Nirṛti was now built in the south-west, and the priest exhorted Nirṛti to seek out as her portion of the sacrifice the men who offer no oblations to the Vedic gods.

(VII. 2.1.1 ff)

To prepare the ground for the great altar, oxen were yoked to a plough and furrows made south, west, north, and east; *kuśa* grass was placed in the middle of the site, the ground was watered by the contents of fifteen jars (VII, 2.4.25), and seeds of several varieties of plants and herbs were sown. One kind of food was omitted from the planting and of that the sacrificer could not eat for the rest of his life. (VII, 2.4.14)[13] Time passed. The plants grew and yielded their harvest which was originally for medicinal purposes, and cures verging on the miraculous were expected.

> Herbs had sprung up three ages earlier than the gods and those which were brown contained one hundred powers and seven. The man who had such a store of herbs was like a king among men, and his name was Physician, he was a slayer of fiends and a chaser of disease. The plants, together with their Sovran Lord Soma, agree to save from death the man whose cure a Brahman undertakes.
>
> (Underlining is mine).
>
> (Precis: Y.V. XII, 75-102)

Such was the intention of the Yajurveda but, when the priests tied the ritual to the Prajāpati myth, the interpretation changed. Instead of healing humans (or perhaps as well as healing humans, for the Brahmins were often referred to as physicians) the plants restored to Prajāpati the strength which had left him at the completion of creation (VII, 2.4.28) so that, in a sense, the priests had produced an elixir of immortality.

The site was covered with sand and, at sunset, a white horse protected it from the enmity of the Rākṣasas. And so, finally, the altar could be built.

Components of the Altar

Since the altar was not built for purposes of community worship as a Westerner would expect, but was the sacrificer's personal altar, a special relationship must be established between himself and Agni/fire altar.

> Now were he [the sacrificer] to build up Agni without taking him up (altar/Agni) into his own self, he would beget man from man, mortal from mortal, one not freed from sin from one not freed from sin; but when he builds up Agni after taking him up into his own self, he causes Agni to be born from Agni, the immortal from the immortal, the sinless from the sinless.
>
> (VII, 4.1.1)

To evoke this rapport the sacrificer prayed:

> Within me I first take Agni. (VII, 4.1.2)

And sang the Satya Sāman:

> For the gods then said: 'Let us make the truth (satya) his mouth (or beginning). (VII, 4.1.3)

In the centre of the altar ground he placed a lotus leaf (VII, 4.1.7), and on the lotus leaf the gold plate from about his neck (VII, 4.1.10), and on this he placed the golden figure of a man (VII, 4.1.15) with the words of R.V., X.121.1:

> In the beginning rose Hiraṇyagarbha born only lord of all created beings,
> He fixeth and holdeth up this earth and heaven, What god shall we adore with our oblations?
>
> Trans. N. Macnicol[14]

Naturally Prajāpati was identified with the "*ka*" of the hymn. (VII, 4.1.19)

The sacrificer then stood by the golden man worshipping him with the Sarpanāma (serpent named) formulas. (VII, 4.1.26) Griffith suggests[15] that a comparison be made with hymns addressed to serpents as powerful super-human beings, and the *brāhmaṇas* do give their commentary this sense, for the formulas are to appease everything in the world which creeps (v. 27): Moreover, serpents are the darts of demons (v. 29) and an all-embracing homage to serpents in all the worlds is thought necessary (v. 30). The word "Sarpanāma" was explained by a play on roots; "the serpents are these worlds for these glide along √*sṛp* (*sarp*)" (VII, 4.1.25) and "because the gods stopped the worlds and caused them to bend √*nam*." (VII, 4.1.26)

"Hiraṇyagarbha" is the golden germ or golden womb, and it is important to understand what was honoured with the central position of the altar, for there can be no doubt that whatever extraordinary power was to be invoked by the ritual, it was meant to concentrate its force upon this central point of the *vedi*.

The lotus leaf, the gold plate, and the golden man as symbols were interpreted by the *brāhmaṇas* as follows:

Of the *lotus leaf* they said:

> It is a womb and the sacrificer places it in the centre as a womb from which Agni may be born. The lotus leaf is the waters and the lotus leaf lies spread on the waters, so the earth lies spread on the waters. The same earth is Agni's womb for Agni the fire altar is the earth, since thereof the whole is built up. . . .
>
> (VII, 4.1.7,8)

Of the *gold plate* they said:

> Gold is fire, light, and immortality. (XIII, 4.1.7) That plate is yonder sun. (VII, 4.1.10)

Of the *golden man* they said:

> He is Prajāpati, is Agni, is the Sacrificer, is made of gold for gold is light, and fire is light: gold is immortality, and fire is immortality. It is a man (puruṣa) for Prajāpati is the Man—the gods called him hiramya, hiramya being what is mystically called hiraṇya (gold). THE GODS LOVE THE MYSTIC.
>
> (VII, 4.1.15, 16)

If the symbols are read progressively they mean that water is the undifferentiated base both for this world and the cosmos, and from the water the lotus leaf arises; the leaf as a womb contains a differentiated form and marks this embryo off from the uncreated; the womb gives birth to the golden man, that is, the perfected man, the divine man who for the purpose of the ceremony is identified as the sacrificer, for the sacrificer's gold initiation plate was placed under the golden man. The gold links the sacrificer with the sun, which is light and fire, the divine wisdom and immortality.

The sacrificer then placed upon the golden man a brick with natural perforations. (VII, 4.2.1) There would be three of these bricks in the altar—representing the earth, air, and sky, and the holes in them would permit the sacrificer to breathe, and to pass through to the eternal abode. Using this first-laid brick as a marker, he then placed another to the east, and in front of that one—two bricks, one on each side of the spine, and, finally, the Aṣāḍhā, the brick which represented his consort. A living tortoise, of which the lower shell was the terrestrial world and the upper shell the world above, was then laid into the altar, facing to the west. (VII, 5.1.1)

All openings in the heads of the sacrificial victims were filled with splinters of gold (VII, 5.2.8) and arranged in a pattern around the firepan. (VII, 5.2.1 ff) We have seen in the Prajāpati myth the importance of the head as the place of excellence; we have also observed that the priests were hesitant to state clearly that their victims were slain, and that they took excessive precautions to avert any unwanted influences which might ruin the outcome of the ritual. To satisfy both these needs now presented the priests with a problem, for they must entomb the heads in the altar for the *śrī* contained therein, but without the aura of burning distress which they believed they had inflicted on the victims when slaughtering them. In order to remove any lingering of pain, certain ritual actions, the *utsargas*, were performed. (VII, 5.2.28) By this means the aura was transferred to live animals (VII. 5.2.32 ff) which were driven away from the sacrificial area and banished to where Parjanya does not rain. (VII, 5.2.37) Was this a scapegoat to the desert ?

Within twelve months the sacrificer will complete the altar by constructing at least four more layers of bricks with layers of earth between them. These layers do not evoke the imagination and, although ritually copious, do not have the creative quality of the first layer. It was recognized that there was a ritual necessity for five layers and therefore there are at least five layers, but (in my opinion) the ritual no longer flows freely and appears laborious and contrived.

Possibly because of this lack of specific dogma the number of layers was variously represented as being five, or six, or seven. Eggeling noted[16] "though the fire-altar is commonly called the five-layered one, consisting as it does of five complete layers of bricks, on the top of these there is a small additional pile of two layers, the lower one in the form of the Gārhapatya hearth, and the upper one, consisting of two bricks, on which the fire is ultimately laid down."

The original intention seems to have been that Prajāpati was restored by the building of five layers of bricks alternating with five layers of earth. The layers of earth were the mortal parts of Prajāpati and the layers of brick, the immortal. This restoration of Prajāpati, which was also the restoration, or the finding of, the immortal self of the sacrificer, caused the layers to be thought to represent parts of a man or Man, so that the first layer was the legs, the second—above the legs and below the waist, the third—the waist, the fourth—above the waist and below the neck, the fifth—the neck and the sixth—the head. (VIII, 7.4.19 ff) The seventh layer was the vital airs (VIII, 7.4.21) so it would seem that the seven layers were contrived to represent the seven *puruṣas* who had formed Prajāpati.

Emphasis was placed on the year in one form or another and seasonal bricks were placed in each layer so that the entire seasonal year could be incorporated in the finished structure. The horizon and the zenith, and the specified abodes of the various gods, demons, and Yama, were incorporated by the laying of regional bricks. Each layer was associated with a part of the universe so that the gods might ascend from earth, to air, to sky, as each layer was completed. The god associated with a particular region was especially important to an appropriate layer, for example: Agni to earth; Vāyu to air; and Āditya-Sūrya to sky. The creation bricks were laid to symbolize the creation of living beings by the self-sacrifice of Prajāpati, and the deliverance bricks were laid because of Prajāpati's deliverance.

As the altar neared completion some of the beauty returned to the ritual for it was said that, when the gods mounted the fourth layer, they saw the far-shining heavens—a place of brilliance, peace, and solidity, and as sympathetic tokens of that vision the sacrificer laid far-shining bricks, foeless bricks, and firmament-seating bricks.

One interpretation of the layers which followed the pattern of world, air, and sky for the first three layers made the fourth layer the sacrifice, and the fifth layer the sacrificer. (VIII, 7.4.12 ff) When the sacrificer had built five layers he completed the altar by sprinkling on it one thousand pieces of gold. (VIII, 7.4.9) This was the sixth layer, the heavenly world.

And so, finally, the sacrificer came to the supreme moment of his ritual. He transferred the sacred fire, which he had been nurturing daily for almost a year, to its central position on the golden altar. The final placement of this fire was the seventh layer, the layer of Immortality. (VIII, 7.4.18) The completed altar was a golden bird, bearing a golden man at its centre, and facing towards the sun.

The Śatarudrīya

As the sacrificer stood with outstretched arms, he and his priests plunged from that contemplation of self-transcendence to the repetition of a tedious litany, the Śatarudrīya (Y.V. XVI; Ś.B., IX), which detailed one hundred forms of Rudra, the god who was violent and terrifying in nature, death and disease-inducing in animal and man. Here is another facet of the syndrome—concurrent with the terror of ritual gone wrong, with respect to the other face of god just in case, with blood sacrifice to the moon, with Nirṛti's blackfaced altar—except that now the golden altar stands completed, a magnet to all the positive elements, and therefore the potential of the negative has also increased, like ever-increasing Vṛtra.

A psychologically sound truth was expressed in this sudden release of an awesome numinous. The sacrificer's mind had been conditioned by almost a year of intense concentration upon, and devotion to, a ritual form. His spiritual awareness had been nurtured for as many months, deliberately withdrawn from any mundane contact. The sacrificer waited on the threshold, his mind and spirit rising, and the subconscious depths must balance such outreaching. Many spiritual geniuses have recorded an awareness of an evil and destructive force whose power greatly increased just prior to a penetration to the mind, intellect, and soul of intense illumination. "The dark night of the soul,"[17] a phase of the inner life experienced by Western mystics as a state of darkness and separation from god, was ritually expressed here. Remember that, though the Agnicayana was an extensive ritual, it was a ritual for one man, and the evil to be averted by libations to Rudra, was to be averted for one man.

Possession of the Altar

When the Śatarudrīya was completed the sacrificer took possession of his altar, covering as much as possible with his outstretched arms. He placed a stone in the junction of the right wing and body, sprinkled the altar with water, then placed the stone in the empty water pitcher, which was then cast away. A frog, a shoot of bamboo, and a lotus-flower (IX, 1.2.20) said to be emblems of coolness, were then drawn across the altar.

The sacrificer mounted his altar and, standing there with outstretched arms, prayed:

To him who dwells in man, Hail!
To him who dwells in waters, Hail!
To him who dwells in sacred grass, Hail!
To him who dwells in the wood, Hail!
To him who finds the light, Hail!

(Y. V. XVII, 12)

When the morning sun rose the sacrificer greeted it as Savitṛ, as he had greeted it twelve months previously at the beginning of the ritual:

Savitar, golden-hued, hath lifted eastward, bright with the sunbeams, his eternal lustre.

He at whose furtherance wise Pūshan marches surveying all existence like a herdsman.

He sits, the measurer, in the midst of heaven, filling the two world-halves and air's mid-region,

He looks upon the rich far spreading pastures between the eastern and the western limit.

Steer, Sea, Read Bird with strong wings, he hath entered the dwelling place of the Primeval Father.

A gay-hued Stone set in the midst of heaven, he hath gone forth and guards the air's two limits.

(Y.V. XVII, 58, 59, 60.)

The sacrificer then set up "a gay-hued stone." A sun-stone as opposed to a moon-stone ? A commemorative stone ? To mark the place of worship? To mark the place of sunrise on that one day of the year ? As an image of the new self ? To prophesy by changing colours? As a symbol of the variegated pebble in the Prajāpati myth? A philosopher's stone intended to be golden in its final form? One single, erect stone could have conveyed any of these meanings.

The priests now prayed for benefits for the sacrificer, commending him to the gods:

To thee I trust this man... After you will the Sacrificer follow. Here recognize him in the highest heaven... When he approacheth by the God-ward pathways, reveal to him the meed of pious actions."

(Y.V. XVIII, 59, 60)

And, finally, the priest pronounced the blessing on the man who had gained Immortality:

Do thou, Most Youthful God, protect the men who offer, hear their songs, protect his offspring and himself.

(Y.V. XVIII, 77)

CHAPTER V

References and Notes

1. Dowson, *A Classical Dictionary of Hindu Mythology*, "Aṅgiras."

2. Ś.B. X, 6.4.9 and also Eggeling, I, xxxi-xxxiii.

3. *The time of the sacrifice in relation to the phases of the moon.* Because both the Ś.B. and the Y.V. are inclined to switch from place to place in the ritual, it was with difficulty that I concluded that the animals used for searching for the clay deposit are not the animals which are slaughtered. Only the horse appears to be necessary for the discovery of the clay deposit, and after the discovery of the clay, all animals are led away.

The Brāhmaṇa states : "thus, then, what first full moon there is (in the year) on that he slaughters the victim; and what first eight day there is, on that he prepares the fire-pan; and what first new moon there is, on that he becomes initiated." (VI, 2.2.30)

Therefore, the ritual must follow one of two courses :

Firstly : Time is calculated from full moon to full moon. One set of animals is slaughtered at the full moon; a second set of animals is used for the search for the clay which begins on the eighth day after full moon; on the new moon, he is initiated.

Alternately : Time is calculated from dark of moon to last quarter of waning moon. At the new moon he is initiated; on the eighth day he searches for the clay, and on the full moon the animals are slaughtered.

Y.V., XI, 55 seems to support this proposition for Sinīvālī, the new-moon goddess, is asked to soften the clay.

4. Compare Sinīvālī with the anima-figure which guides the dead man across the Cinvat Bridge. *The Vision of Arda Viraf* cited by Campbell, *Occidental Mythology*, p. 193 ff.

And also :

Bal Gangadhar Tilak, *Orion—or Researches into the Antiquity of the Vedas* (Extract, British Museum, 1893). Tilak identified the Vedic gate-equinoxes, sacrificial posts, and two dogs as guardians with the Iranian gate-Chinvat Bridge, and the dogs which protect the bridge. He then proved that the vernal equinox was near the Dog Star in those days, thus making the Dog rise with the sun at the beginning of the year, at the gates of the sacrifice.

5. Dutt, *A History of Civilization in Ancient India* I, Chapter VII. Dutt gives a resumé of development of astronomy with Vedic and Brahmanic references, seasons, phases of the moon, the Nakṣatras; presents the controversial opinions surrounding the indigenous development of the Lunar Zodiac.

6. Cirlot, *Symbols*, p. 145.
7. Eggeling, Part III, p. 265, fn. 2.
8. Ibid, p. 269, fn. 3.
9. Zimmer : *Myths and Symbols in Indian Art and Civilization*, p. 154.
10. Eggeling I, p. 88, fn. 2, citing Haug's commentary on Ait.B. 3, 8.
11. Macdonell : *A Vedic Reader*, p. 31.
12. *New Larousse Encyclopedia of Mythology*, p. 337.
13. A. P. Elkin, *The Australian Aborigines*, especially Chapter IX. A comparison may be made with the aborigine's refusal to eat of his totem, whereby a mutual, spiritual relationship and inter-dependence was established between man and nature.
14. N. Macnicol : *Hindu Scriptures*.
15. Griffith : *Yajurveda*, p. 137, fn. 5.
16. Ibid, III, p. 249, fn. 3.
17. S. Spencer, *Mysticism in World Religions*, p. 251.

CHAPTER VI

THE AGNICAYANA III

An Analysis of the Altar Design

The text of the Śatapatha Brāhmaṇa which concerned itself with the Agnicayana was commentary upon the ritual itself; therefore, the fact that the tenth *kāṇḍa* which immediately follows, was a further elucidation based on mystical speculation, appears to indicate that certain ideas could not easily be inserted into the original commentary. (X, 1.1.3)

This tenth *kāṇḍa* purports to explain the mystery of the fire altar but, if this is so, a further chapter should have been written to explain the explanation. The compiler or compilers of the *kāṇḍa* experienced no discomfort in placing within the *kāṇḍa* points of view which were incompatible; however, they did present some coherent material related to the Agnicayana. Especially they emphasized: (1) the multiple cross-identification of the creation legend, the vital airs, Prajāpati, Agni, the fire altar, the three worlds, the year, the sacrificer, and the metres of the hymns; (2) the identification of Prajāpati with the Puruṣa of the Ṛgvedic hymn, so that it became Prajāpati whom the gods first sacrificed (X, 2.2.1, 2); (3) details of seasons, times, distances on the sacrificial ground; and (4) a continuing interest in magical numbers, especially 7 and 101 (X, 2.4.4 ff and X, 2.6.10 ff) and 720. The number, 720, was expressed as: $360\times2:3\times80\times3:180\times4:144\times5:120\times6:90\times8:80\times9:72\times10:60\times12:16\times45:18\times40:20\times36:24\times30$ (X, 4.2.1-17), which is an excellent example of their practical application of numbers.

Positive statements were made of the expectations of the man who had built the fire altar. Some of these were of a material nature, such as fame, fortune, and well-being; generally the sacrificer sought immortality. We can see from the multiplicity of speculation that interpretation was not yet a closed book.

Dr. P. N. Chopra of New Delhi has informed me (Dec.' 74)[1] in answer to my enquiry, that no fire altar has been found in archaeological surveys in India. This means that all statements by scholars regarding the design of the altar, the size of it, and the materials used in its construction, and the appearance of the finished altar, must be inferred from literary sources, and from such inferences, conclusions have been made regarding the religious intention of the *brāhmaṇas*.

Eggeling[2] calculated that 10,800 bricks (i.e., *lokampṛṇā*= space-filler) were used in building the altar, that the body measured 400 square feet, each wing 120 square feet, and the tail 110 square feet. There is no doubt that the *brāhmaṇas* thought of the altar as bird-shaped (the original fire container was bird-shaped because the embryo is the shape of that which will be born from it) and the final shape may have looked like this :

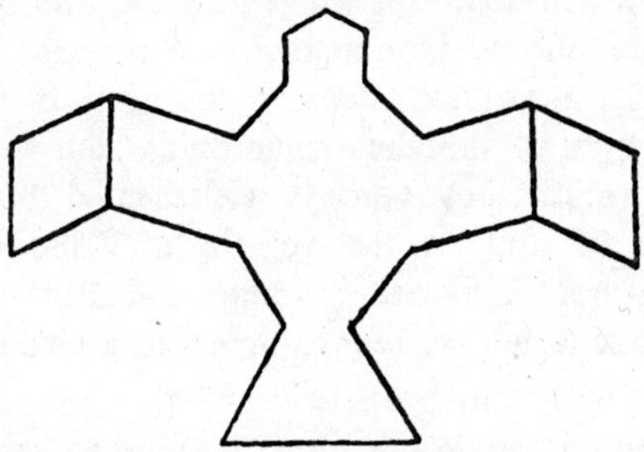

(Plan of the altar in the shape of a Falcon, after G. Thibaut)[3]

A comparison may be made with Persian archaeological evidence as, for instance, this carving of Ahura Mazda which has wings and tail but a human head.

(Ahura Mazda, the god of the Archaemenid kings of Persia, carved in relief at Pesepolis)[4]

The fire altar could also have been bird-shaped with a human head at the centre or with a human body (the golden man) in the centre. We have seen that when the seven *puruṣas* combined to form Prajāpati, Prajāpati's form could have been that of a human, a winged celestial being, or a bird. Since the head, as the seat of *śrī* was specifically mentioned, it is more likely that his shape tended towards human rather than bird form.

The bird shape of the altar has been likened to a hawk, falcon, or eagle, birds traditionally associated with the sun, for it was thought that they flew almost to the sun itself and yet, miraculously it seemed, were not burnt by the sun's rays. Icarus, in the tradition of the man with wings, flew too close to the sun and the wax which held his wings in place was melted by the heat of the sun and he plummetted into the sea. Special rites "cooled" the fire-altar and attention was given by the priests to the joints which were thought to manipulate the wings (X, 2.1.1 ff.) In Indian mythology Garuḍa represented this part-eagle, part-human motif and, as the vehicle of Viṣṇu, expresses the same bird-sun-man association. The Mahaduktham, Great Litany, was made (laboriously) analogous to a bird shape.[5]

Another ruin with which I believe the altar may be compared is that of an Achaemenian fire altar, thought to have been built about the 6th century B.C. and excavated near Cyrus's capital of Pasargadae.

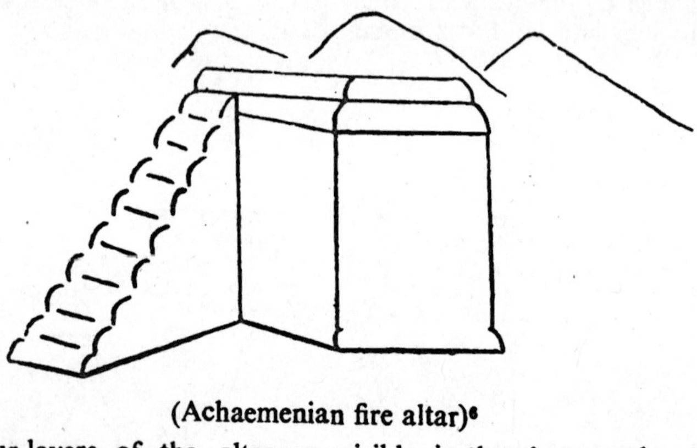

(Achaemenian fire altar)[6]

Four layers of the altar are visible in the photograph, and more may be obscured by the earth around the base. Since the

Śatapatha Brāhmaṇa records that both the sacrificer and the gods mounted the altar, possibly the Brahmanic altar also had a set of steps. One would assume that the sacrificer mounted the steps and stood with his back to them and, if this were so, when standing on the Achaemenian altar he would be facing cliffs of a desolate hill, whereas the Agnicayana site must have an unobstructed view eastward.

On the basis of examinations of pottery techniques disclosed by archaeological surveys in India, H. S. Converse[7] has speculated that the Agnicayana rite was indigenous (i.e., of Harappan origin), having been adapted by the *brāhmaṇas* from local culture. To support his view he submits evidence that: (a) the Harappans used millions of fired bricks, but the Ṛgveda did not even have a word for "brick"; (b) the building of the fire altar was the only rite which used bricks, the other altars being of packed earth; and (c) the fire-pan was to be fired with the bottom turned up, and this inverted firing technique characterized the black and red ware of the indigenous non-Vedic culture.

Although there is sufficient literary evidence (tradition of a separate line of teachers, moon and sun times, goddesses at the beginning and the alien Rudra at the end of the ritual) to make one aware that the Agnicayana was different from the usual ritual, yet there is also too much Vedic content for it to have originated other than in the society whose culture we call Aryan.

The word used for "brick" in the Śatapatha Brāhmaṇa was *iṣṭakā*. "Inasmuch as he saw them after offering (istva) the animal, therefore they are bricks (istaka)." (VI, 2.1.10) A brick made before, or without animal sacrifice was *aniṣṭakā*. Eggeling observed that this was a play on words for *aniṣṭakā* may mean either "non-bricks" or "being without oblation."[8] It could be that the fired brick was used only for this fire altar (as Converse suggests) or that a distinction was always made between the sacred and secular use of bricks.

According to the *brāhmaṇas*, clay and water were the composition of a brick, and the brick was identified with the "self," thus: "I shall become a mortal carcase, not freed from evil; well then, I will bake it by means of the fire." (VI, 2.1.9) The baking of the brick is then regarded as a purificatory rite, for, if the sacrificial food when baked becomes immortal, then the bricks when baked become immortal. (VI, 2.1.9)

From the evidence above, the *brāhmaṇas* clearly understood the distinction between baked and unbaked bricks, but it may be that the *brāhmaṇas* had no brickmaking skills (that was not their function in the society) and that, in changing from earth to brick altars, they copied the techniques of better tradesmen. A lack of skill in the brickmaking (for instance, in the bonding material) could explain the absence of archaeological evidence.

If we accept the bird shape as a description of the finished altar but set aside other inferences, and concentrate our attention on the plan of the first layer, the layer to which the *brāhmaṇas* gave most attention, and which the remaining layers must necessarily follow—then the bricks of the first layer were placed about the symbolic objects in the centre as in the following diagram:

Diagram of First Layer

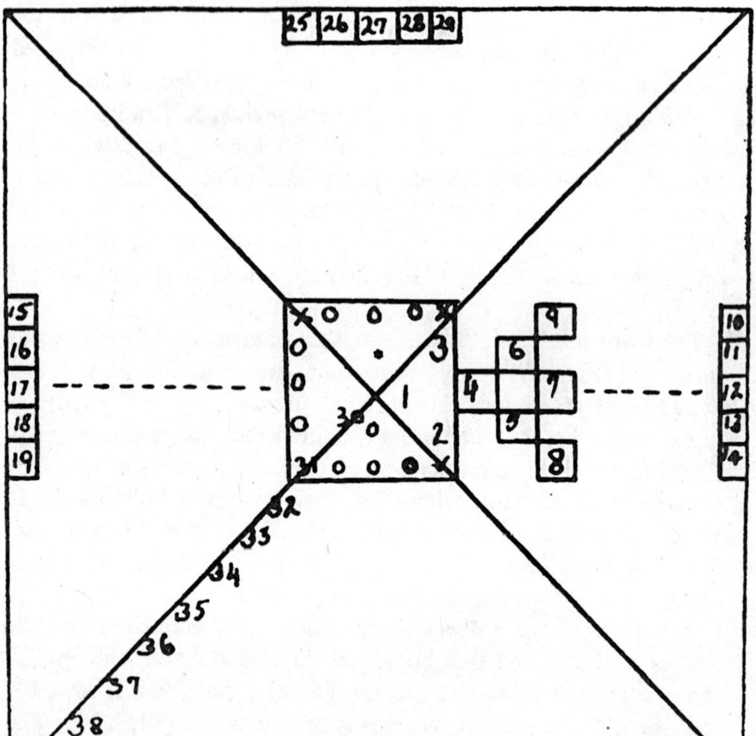

*lotus leaf, plate, man, porous brick.

1. Dviyajus brick (because two deities saw it).
2 & 3. Retaḥsic (seed shedders).
4. Viśvajyotiṣ (all-light).
5 & 6. Ṛtavyā (seasonal).
7. Asāḍhā.
8. Live tortoise.
9. Wooden mortar and pestle; firepan; heads of victims.
10, 11, 12, 13, 14. Apasyā (water bricks).
15, 16, 17, 18, 19. "
20, 21, 22, 23, 24 "
25, 26, 27, 28, 29 "
30 to 39. Prāṇabhṛt (breath-holders).

I have supposed that, since five bricks are centred on the four sides of the square, that the centre brick of these five bricks was the line of the spine and that, therefore, the spine was represented by the width of a brick. This also permits one brick to be placed in the centre of the altar. The ten bricks would then be placed in the centre as a small square.

Eggeling supposed that the spines (the lines running north-south and east-west, and meeting at the centre) were "thin" lines, that is, the "line" is the jointing of two rows of bricks. Eggeling expressed doubt as to the exact placement of the ten inner bricks, but in this diagram of the central part of the first layer, it can be seen that Eggeling's pattern forms a circle (as opposed to my square).[9]

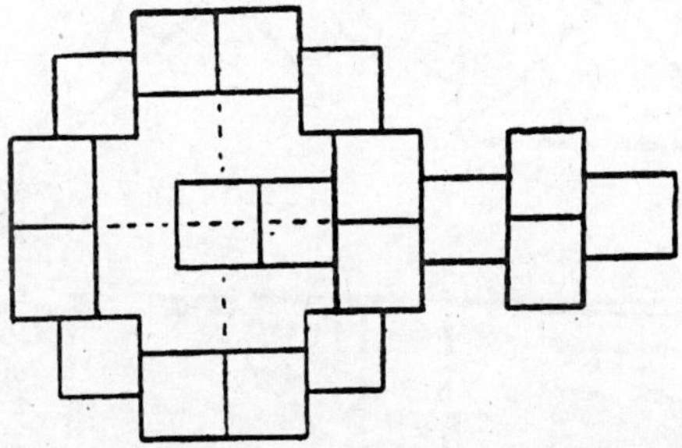

If we examine the patterns which surround the centre of the layer (and forget the bird which the layer might become), the following patterns emerge as being part of the whole design, and each pattern can be identified as a specific graphic symbol.

	Altar diagram with part shaded	*Part as Graphic*	*Description*
1.	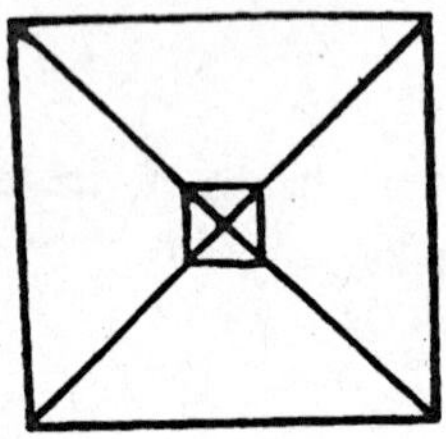		Centre of altar as square.
2.		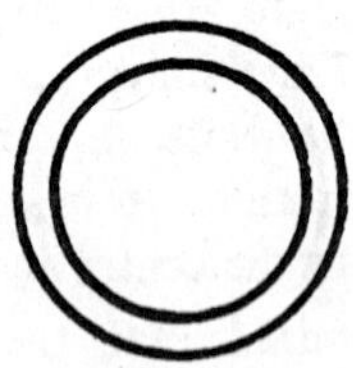	ff. Eggeling: a maṇḍala; a circle within a circle.
3.		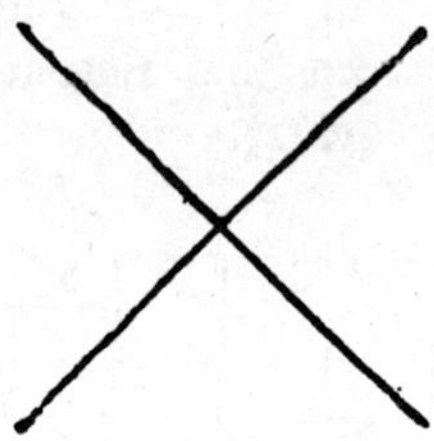	Square divided into four.
4.	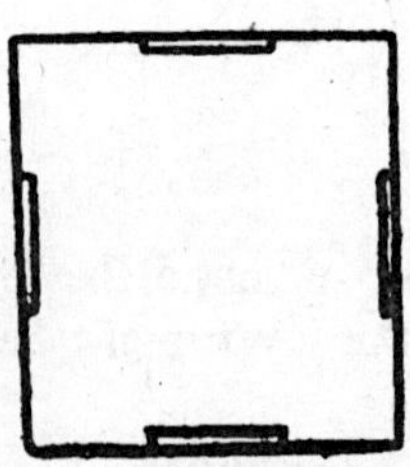	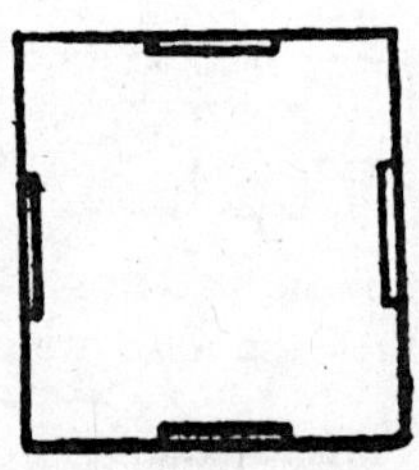	Square : with four entrances: cf. patterns of temples, cit :,Garden of Eden.

	Altar diagram	*Part as Graphic*	*Description*
5			Two triangles; these are the graphics for fire and water, evolution and involution.
6	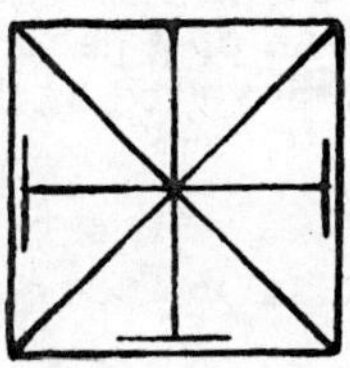	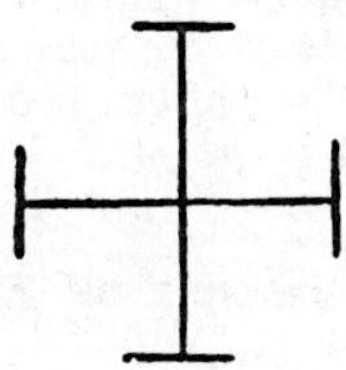	A form of swastika. This graphic combines both left-handed and right-handed swastikas, perhaps intentionally representing the increasing and decreasing seasons of the sun. Also North, South, East, West.
7			Sun-wheel or lotus, 8-spoked, or 8-petalled. The figure 8 signifies the intersection of earth and heaven.

It is not intended to press the comparison, but I believe it is relevant that the numerals of the Prajāpati myth are repeated in these graphics, for example: four, six, eight.

Since we now have graphics from primitive societies as well as from the àrts of Eastern and Western cultures,[10] each outline is a familiar representation, and a comparative analysis of each is possible. From such an analysis, we can see that Brahmanic choice fell upon graphics symbolic of the Centre, the Poles, or the Sun, but never on a symbol for the moon or the stars, even though the two triangles differently placed could have formed a six-pointed star. The *brāhmaṇas* intuitively had produced diagrams which were perfect for their purpose. In both Buddhism and Hinduism diagrams became devotional aids. As Zimmer observed:

> In Hindu devotional tradition *yantra* is the general term for instruments of worship, namely, idols, pictures, or geometrical diagrams. A *yantra* may serve as.... a kind of a chart or schedule for the gradual evolution of a vision, while identifying the Self with its slowly varying contents, that is to say, with the divinity in all its phases of transformation. In this case the *yantra* contains dynamic elements.
>
> We may say, then, that a *yantra* is an instrument designed to curb the psychic forces by concentrating them on a pattern, and in such a way that this pattern becomes reproduced by the worshipper's visualizing power.[11]

The *yantra* used as an example by Zimmer as a geometrical design was the Śrī-Yantra.

The Śrī-Yantra[12]

This *yantra* embodies forms which are either totally identical with, or very similar to, those forms basic to the diagram of the fire altar. For example:

1. With the enclosing outline of a square with four entrances (Śrī-Yantra)
   Compare figures 1 and 4 on p. 98.
2. With the circle contained within a square (Śrī-Yantra)
   Compare figure 2 on p. 98.
3. With the design of triangles which is a complex design based on two triangles (Śrī-Yantra)
   Compare figure 5 on p. 99.
4. With the two circles of lotus petals, the inner one of which has eight petals (Śrī-Yantra)
   Compare figure 7 on p. 99.

In fact, the only design in the fire altar not contained in the Śrī-Yantra is that in figure 3, p. 98, and it is possible that these were originally guidelines for finding the central point of the altar site.

There had to come a day when a ritual as elaborate as the Agnicayana should lose its popularity, either because the culture was no longer materially capable of producing such wealth among the *brāhmaṇas*, or because those who would normally perform it questioned its merit. History asserts that the priests so over-ritualized that the performance became tedious; the truth of such a tendency is recorded for all time in the priests' own words. History also asserts that the Brahmins lost their domination, externally to two movements—Jainism and Buddhism—and internally to the philosophy of the Upaniṣads.

It is not my intention to claim that the maṇḍalas of Buddhism, especially in Tibet, or the *yantras* of Hinduism had their origins in the diagrams of the sacrificial system. However, I would wish to reverse that statement and say that, when a time came in which it was no longer possible to build a fire altar, may it not have been possible to achieve the same results by representing the fire altar diagrammatically?

CHAPTER VI

References and Notes

1. Dr. P. N. Chopra, Dr. Zakir Husain Marg, New Delhi. Personal letter.

2. Eggeling : Part IV, p. 352, fn. 1.

3. Illustrated by Renou, *Vedic India*, after G. Thibaut, Journal of the Asiatic Society of Bengal, 1875.

4. Drawing from a photograph, *New Larousse Encyclopedia of Mythology*, p. 292.

5. Eggeling, Part IV, xxvii.

6. Drawing from a photograph, *New Larousse Encyclopedia of Mythology*, p. 310.

7. H.C. Converse, "The Agnicayana Rite: Indigenous Origins?," *History of Religions*, Vol. XIV, 2, 1974-75, p. 81.

8. Eggeling, Part III, p. 164, fn. 2.

9. Ibid., Part IV, p. 16, fn. 2.

10. For example, see Cirlot, *Symbols*, also Andreas Lommel, *Prehistoric and Primitive Man*.

11. Zimmer, *Myths and Symbols in Indian Art and Civilization*, p. 141.

12. Ibid : Plate 36

CHAPTER VII

DIVINE REALITY

What then was the divine reality which the *brāhmaṇas* expressed, described, or realized in the Śatapatha Brāhmaṇa? There can be no simple answer for, although divine reality cannot alter, the Indian viewpoint has been that manifestations of divine reality vary according to the spiritual needs or the receptivity of the individual. The *brāhmaṇas* acted in the tradition of worship . . . and let worship,* which was to become one of the most distinctive features of Hinduism and, therefore, the *brāhmaṇas* knew divine reality in many forms. The complexity of the ritual is self-evident, and each ritual should not be denied the right to stand as a self-sufficient entity defining one pathway by which man sought to find, and to express, divine reality.

The Old Gods: A Theistic[3] Relationship

We have witnessed the glory of divine reality in the splendour of the sacrificial ritual—material splendour in the accoutrements, poetic splendour in the use of Vedic hymns, mythical and legendary splendour in the 1001 stories, and creative and artistic splendour in the pageantry of ritual actions. The materialistic also served as symbolic manifestations of apparently unrelated divine or sacred objects—*soma* stalks as King Soma, the golden man as Prajāpati or the sacrificer, the tortoise as earth and sky—to name only a few. Underlying these

*A developing tradition of non-interference with an individual's spiritual competence formed a religious *laissez-faire* "live . . . and let live" hence "worship . . . and let worship."

was a state of mind which took certain things for granted—man is sinful, god is sinless;[3] both the duration of and the place of, the sacrifice are sacred; the sacrificer's personality will change; no deity is represented by a model or statue; the concept of divine reality is never limited to one form; communion with the divine was by means of a communal cup or meal partaken either on the sacrificial ground or at the hearth fire.

Divine reality was at least the old gods of the Ṛgveda for these were named, had offerings and libations sent to them and were addressed personally in prayers and hymns. The dominant theological expression of the Vedic period was the theistic relationship between god and man.[4] In such a relationship a man may experience god's essence, as in the beatific vision, or the mystery, influence, even companionship of god but, in terms of his soul or personality or mind, man forever stands apart from god.

The eternity of the divine was displayed in the concept of time illustrated by the mind-reducing estimates of the immensity of just one Yuga. The destruction of mankind by the flood reminded man of god's omnipotence and mankind's insignificance. The divine was apprehended in the beauty of natural manifestations as, for example, in the sun rising over the sacrificial ground. If god made man in his own image (and Prajāpati did if like produces like) then man has something of the divine in his nature. Divinity so permeated all creation that, not only did chthonic and hostile forces exercise power as real as that of the beneficent powers, but woman's fertility and man's virility were potent forces which could be stimulated by the creative divine.

Death and the Afterlife

The *brāhmaṇas* naturally inherited all of these Vedic traditions since they were part of the Yajurvedic component of the Vedic literature, but they then introduced the Prajāpati myth into their interpretation of the Agnicayana. This would not have had far-reaching effects had it not eroded the belief in a personal participation in an afterlife with Yama, for all men, by counter-claiming immortality for only a few men who, through an aggregate of birth and circumstances, were able to perform the

Agnicayana. Even the death ritual for the man who had performed the Agnicayana differed from usual practice and included the raising of a mound-grave, similar in outline to the altar; when his flesh was cremated the bones were placed amongst bricks to form a birdlike pattern (XIII, 8.3.9).

The *brāhmaṇas* clearly expressed what they hoped to attain by performing the sacrifice.

> By certain ritual actions Prajāpati became immortal; and in like manner does the Sacrificer become immortal by making that body (of the altar) immortal.
>
> (X, 1.3.7)

And again:

> And in like manner does the Sacrificer now finally make a golden form for his body; and inasmuch as (he does so) finally, this is the final form of his body; and, hence, whether they know this or not, people say that the Agnikit (he who has built an altar) is born in yonder world as one made of gold.
>
> (X, 1.4.9)

And yet again:

> By building the altar 'the Sacrificer conquers recurring death'.
>
> (X, 1.4.14)

But what is immortality? The assurance of eternal life, or the assurance of a limited period of bliss in a heavenly[5] situation? What is "yonder world"? The one outside one's window? Or one beyond the furthest sun? Or a spiritual state? And what is recurring death? The *brāhmaṇas* sought their own answers and a new type of speculation entered into the Brāhmaṇa, recorded by individuals in isolated passages without, at first, forming any type of total pattern. Especially each pondered the question: With what did one survive death and enjoy immortality? Even Prajāpati was half-mortal and half-immortal and his mortal half feared Death.' (X, 1.3.2) Again, Prajāpati (as a sort of divine prototype) consisted of a clear-cut dichotomy: Prajāpati's vital airs were immortal, and his body mortal. (X, 1.4.1) Therefore, given the juxtaposition of the body (mortal) and the vital airs/*prāṇa* (immortal), speculation followed as to what in man might be mortal, what immortal.

> Five forms are mortal; the hair on the mouth, the skin, the flesh, the bone, and the marrow; and these are immortal—the mind, the voice, the vital airs, the eye, and the ear.
>
> (X, 1.3.4)

It is apparent that the first group is tangible, physical; the second group is comprised of intangibles, or, more correctly, an intangible quality exists behind a physical one—man's mind within the brain; sight within the eye.

We have witnessed the Brahmins' neurotic concern with the death of the animal, their rejection of the fact of the slaughter, their observation that life departed with the breath, and their concern with the revitalizing of the animal. At some time, the human emphasis changed from 'how to live my life' to 'how to die my death.' Moreover, there had to be a defined moment, a definite symptom, which satisfactorily delineated the time of death. It had been claimed for the Brahmins that they were the finest physicians amongst the priests (XIV, 2.2.19) and amidst various ruminations on etymological possibilities (X, 5.2.11 ff) these physician/priests recorded:

> These vital airs (prāṇa) are his own (sva): and when he sleeps (svapiti) then these vital airs take possession of him as his own (svâ api-yanti): hence (the term) 'svâpyaya (being taken possession of by one's own people),' 'svâpyaya' doubtless being what they mystically call 'svapna (sleep),' for the gods love the mystic.
>
> (Underlining is mine) (X, 5.2.14)

Is it pushing meaning too far to see these 'own people' as the images which 'people' the individual's dreaming? That they had no relationship to the waking state is indicated by the verse which follows:

> And when he is asleep, he does not, by means of them, know of anything whatever, nor does he form any resolution with his mind, or distinguish the taste of food with (the channel of) his speech, or distinguish any smell with his breath; neither does he see with his eye, nor hear with his ear, for these (vital airs) have taken possession of him.
>
> (Underlining is mine.) (X, 5.2.15)

The sense perceptions which we have witnessed the *brāhmaṇas* seeking as immortal are here considered in relation to sleep, and possibly the *brāhmaṇas* sensed the direction of their thoughts for the next verse discusses death.[6]

It was also in the tenth *kāṇḍa* that the *brāhmaṇas* made use of the literary device, the theological dispute or discussion between a *brāhmaṇa* and a *rājā* in which the *rājā* usually scored off the *brāhmaṇa*. In one such debate Dhīra Śataparṇeya and Mahāśāla Jābāla discussed the immortal parts and the how of their survival after death. (X, 3.3.1-8)

Their discourse began by affirming that knowledge of Agni increased the power or quality of the sense perception of each immortal part so that, for example, the man who knows Agni as speech becomes eloquent (X,3.3.11), but this may be too pedestrian a way of interpreting their meaning. It was probably the intention to convey that the man with this knowledge of Agni was supranormal. When the faculty of sight is intensified beyond the ordinary we speak of "foresight," "insight," and the idea is perfectly described in the East by "the third eye."

The discussion between the two men then hinged on "The Agni who is everything here." On hearing that Dhīra Śataparṇeya had this knowledge Mahāśāla Jābāla became his student: "Teach me that Agni, sir." (X, 3.3.5)

> He said: "Verily, that Agni is the breath; for when man sleeps, speech passes into the breath, and so do the eye, the mind, and the ear; and when he awakes, they again issue from the breath. Thus much as to the body.
>
> (X, 3.3.6)

The immortal parts of man were then identified with parts of the universe—the eye with sun, mind with the moon, ear with the quarters, breath with the wind. Using the analogy that fire, when it expires, is wafted upwards on the wind, so also the man who *knows* at death has his immortal breath borne on the wind, and all immortal parts are returned to their various sources.

> And when he who knows this passes away from this world, he passes into the fire by his speech, into the sun by his eye, into

> the moon by his mind, into the quarters by his ear, and into the wind by his breath; and being composed thereof, he becomes whichever of these deities he chooses, and is at rest.
> (X, 3.3.8)

It is possible to perceive here an endeavour to make tangible a belief in some immortal part which survives death. The parts which were thought to survive were the physical evidence of life (breath), or bases of sense perception (eye and ear), or the mind —which even modern science cannot pin down to any specific part of the brain, and which, as the power to think about and react to external situations, is the most distinctive part of an individual personality. But a theory which sends each part of a man in a different direction after death does not appear to be suggesting the survival of an individual personality. The dead man may choose the source into which he will surrender himself and, as the end result of his mergence into that source, he is promised "rest" (X, 3.3.8)—which seems to me to offer meagre consolation, and is a favourite cliche in Western funeral jargon.

In these speculations the *brāhmaṇas* have not yet presented the possibility that man has a soul (in the sense of being a bearer of human personality as well as immortality) nor the companion idea that, if all men have such a soul, under what conditions and in what realms would this soul continue to live?[7] These ideas were incipient in another train of speculation centred on the sun.

> In the early *kāṇḍas* the sun had been identified with Death:
> Now yonder burning (sun) doubtless is no other than Death: and because he is Death, therefore the creatures that are on this side of him die. But those that are on the other side of him are the gods, and they are therefore immortal.
> (II, 3.3.7)

The verse continues by describing the rays (*raśmi*) of the sun as being attached to all living creatures, thereby giving to each the vital airs. A very similar idea had been presented in Ancient Egypt where the art of Akenaten's period shows the sun-disc producing rays which extend into hands bearing the *ankh*, the symbol of eternal life. Most representations of Egyptian gods include the *ankh* symbol.

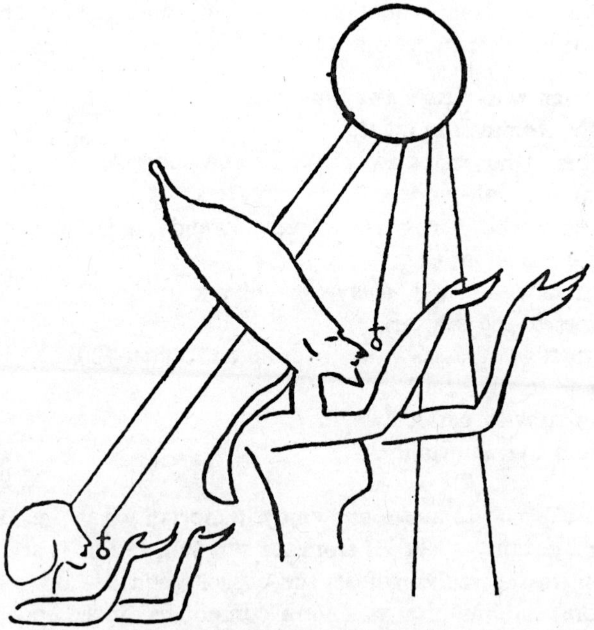

(Akenaten and Nefertiti being proferred *ankh*-symbol on sun rays)[8]

According to the *brāhmaṇas*, when the sun withdrew a ray from an individual, thus causing the loss of the vital airs, the individual died.

> And the breath of whomsoever he (the sun) wishes he takes and rises, and that one dies.
>
> (II, 3.3.8)

The sun's obvious function is to give light and life to the world; nature's function is to absorb sunlight. Because the sun's function was associated mystically with the breath of life, the capacity to absorb sunlight was seen as the reason why some plants, animals and men were long-lived, for the men to whom the sun gave most, lived longest. (X, 2.6.5) Therefore, immortal light/life was attained either by building the 101-fold altar or by living 100 years, and that is why "People say, 'The life of a hundred years makes for heaven'." (X, 2.6.7) Consequently, according to the number of years of one's life, one can attain a certain amount of sunlight, and the amount of this light/life determines one's existence after death.

The man who passes away under 20
goes to day and night.
The man who passes away over 20 and under 40
goes to half-moons.
The man who passes away over 40 and under 60
goes to months.
The man who passes away over 60 and under 80
goes to the seasons.
The man who passes away over 80 and under 100
goes to the year.
The man who passes away over 100
goes to immortality.

(X, 2.6.8)

One's capacity to attain and enjoy immortality was thus based upon immortality absorbed from the sun and, in one's afterlife, one went to the realm whose sun-capacity equalled one's own. Therefore, the immortal was not a component of the body, but was projected into the body from an external source which was capable of withdrawing its essence back into its own nature. Death was once only; at death, one's own sunlight/immortality returned to its source. Again, it was not a survival of an individual personality.

One man recalled the words of the Vedic *ṛṣi*: "There was then neither the non-existent nor the existent" (R.V. X, 129.1) and he described creation as the Mind made manifest:

Mind created speech,
Speech created breath,
Breath created the eye,
Eye created ear,
Ear created work (ritual?)
Work created fire.

(Precis: X, 5.3.3-10)

Thus, all means of sense perception and the practice of ritual based on fire as a means of attaining the immortal senses were derived from an eternal Mind which existed before creation. If this man had then reasoned that recognition of one's self as part of this emanation was divine reality, then death would have meant re-absorption into the Mind.

Both the Sun-projection-and-return and the Mind-projection-and-return belonged to a concept of the diffusion of divine reality which is totally unrelated to theistic theology, and would again appear to be expressive of a minority viewpoint. It was overshadowed by the need to rationalize the fact of the sacrificer's natural death after the building of the fire altar had reputedly earned him immortality, and this need gave rise to a different emphasis.

Originally Prajāpati had taught the gods to lay the altar bricks so that the gods, too, might become immortal. (X, 4.3.8) (One wonders why the gods were not already immortal since immortality appears to be a pre-requisite for being a god.) Moreover, Death assumed that once the gods had this knowledge all men would become immortal and he, therefore, asked:

> 'What share will be mine?'
>
> In response the gods decreed:
>
> 'Henceforward no one shall be immortal with the body; only when thou [Death] shalt have taken that (body) as thy share, he who is to become immortal either through knowledge, or through holy work, shall become immortal after separating from the body.
>
> (Underlining is mine.) (X, 4.3.9)

Now to hold such a belief implies that all humans have a "soul" inhabiting the human body, but distinct from it, so that the body can be subject to Death without injuring the "soul" or, conversely, so that the "soul" can separate from the body. Presumably each soul had a personality which distinguished it from other souls, that is, an individual personality survived after death.

To achieve immortality, the soul must be that of a man who had acquired a certain knowledge or performed certain holy works during his lifetime. Because this theory was being xpoun[illegible] by ritualists of the Agnicayana, the "knowledge" was the secret, mystical knowledge of the Agnicayana, and "holy works" its correct ritual procedure. Although immortality was associated with the man who had performed the Agnicayana, the implication is that all men have an eternal soul, the ability of the soul to arrive at immortality being dependent on a qualitative assessment (by an unknown, or unstated factor) of the man's thoughts and actions during his lifetime. I do not mean to imply that a "judgment" takes place, however, a distinction must be made by something between those who are qualified for immortality, and those who are not. Therefore:

> They who know this, or they who do this holy work, come to life again when they have died, and coming to life, they come to immortal life.
>
> (X. 4.3.10.)

This proposition brought with it a dilemma, for the man who had died to become food for Death, by not performing the Agnicayana (and that must have included many powerful, influential, and holy people in the community; for example, the Buddha, as a *kṣatriya*, could not have performed the Agnicayana) had also an eternal soul, therefore the soul-residue which remained after Death had taken his body, and with which the Agnicit would enjoy immortality, must continue to exist for all other men. The destiny of such men was to be that "they... come to life again when they die, and they become the food of him (Death) time after time." (X, 4.3.10)

I believe here is every reason for attributing to this statement the expression of a belief in re-incarnation, for to speak of re-death instead of re-birth is simply to reverse the emphasis.

> Verily there are deaths connected with all the worlds; and were he not to offer oblations to them, Death would get hold of him in every world.
>
> (XIII, 3.5.1.)

The sense of the passage seems to be clear enough if the doctrine of re-incarnation is accepted. If not accepted, tenuous meanings have to be surmised as indicated by Eggeling who quotes Sāyaṇa as saying that the multi Deaths were "death in the shape of disease, death in the shape of poverty, etc."[9] Neurotic indeed would be the oblation offerer who believed he could ward off death by nominating, and thus eliminating, every means of dying. In view of the presence of a number of worlds in the speculations of the Brāhmaṇa, and of *lokas* in Hinduism and Buddhism, I think it is possible to read the passage as affirming death (and thus life) in spheres other than this world. The oblation offerer may have believed that it was only as a human that he could influence progressive states of existence. Since *Death* is the operative word, what meanings were attached to it?

Death was identified with the *man in the sun* (X, 5.2.3) and all creatures this side of the sun were subject to Death. (We have to assume that the *brāhmaṇas* had no knowledge of other galaxies and that terms like "world beyond the sun" were not statements of factual knowledge).

Death was created by Prajāpati. "Prajāpati created living beings, the gods and mortals, and above the (mortal) beings he created death as their consumer." (X, 1.3.1).

Death was the year "for the year measures life" (X, 4.3.1), and on the same note of Death as a reckoner of time and the days (as is the sun): "it is he who, by day and night, reaches the end of the life of mortals, and then they die." (X, 4.3.2)

The European mediaeval representations of a personified Death always contained a symbol of time, frequently an hourglass.

Death was the portal to immortality. "Within Death is Immortality—for below Death is Immortality—founded on Death is Immortality." (X, 5.2.4)

These references can only be thought of as referring to Death as the end of life in a world in which time is measured by the sun. Therefore, Prajāpati and all Prajāpati's creatures (humans and gods) had a body subject to Death and an eternal "soul" immune from Death. Right knowledge and action released the souls of some via the portals of Death to immortality. The remainder were subject to re-Death (and therefore re-birth) in a world related to Death/Sun/Time, or possibly to rebirth in other *lokas*.

Brahman

Divine reality was also expressed by the word "Brahman." In one passage (XI, 2.3.1 ff) Eggeling specifically defined the word he wanted to use as Brahman (*neuter*) accompanied by the pronoun "*It*." In relating the same myth Dowson used Brahma (*neuter*) as the counterpart of the word used in the Śatapatha Brāhmaṇa.[10]

In essence, this Brahman (n) creation myth states that in the beginning this (universe) was the Brahman (n). *It* made the gods and having created them, It made them ascend these worlds: Agni (earth) Vāyu (air) and Sūrya (sky). It then made higher deities to ascend to higher worlds. (XI, 2.3.1) The Brahman Itself then went up to the sphere beyond and considered how to descend again into these worlds. It descended. . . by means of these two, form and name, and so far as name and form extend, so far extends the universe (XI, 2.3.3).

> These, name and form, are the two great forces of the Brahman and verily, he who knows these two great forces of the Brahman becomes himself a great force.
>
> (XI, 2.3.4)

The myth then states that, in the beginning, the gods were no immortal and did not become so until they were possessed of Brahman. (XI, 2.3.6) Presumably, that was also the way of man's salvation.

Theological Viewpoints

These speculations regarding divine reality and man's relation to it, with which the *brāhmaṇas* were attempting to enter a new era, have finally rested on two theological viewpoints and a fusion of the two.

Firstly, there is the theistic viewpoint in which a god created the world and man has a continuing I-Thou relationship with god expressed in any divine form. I think it is reasonable to state that this was the major emphasis in the Vedic period. The second viewpoint is that divine reality emanates, rather than creates, and so pervades creation that all creation is part of divine reality.[11] This view, found less often in the Ṛgveda, emerged in the Śatapatha Brāhmaṇa as a rather muted expression of divine reality, as diffusion of the Sun or Mind into the created world. The Brahman (n) has combined these two viewpoints—

the first by making Brahman the creator, and the second by the emanation of Brahman as name and form. Brahman is therefore not only the creator of the phenomenal world, but its pervader as well.

This Brahman synthesis resulted in a theological viewpoint, that of the Brahman-Ātman relationship, which was so radically different from what might be expected in writings on sacrificial ritual, that the new theology formed a collection of its own, the Upaniṣads, and the fact that the Śatapatha Brāhmaṇa had provided the means of transition was obscured. It would be impossible to nominate step by step the emergence of such a doctrine, but the evidence is surely there in the beliefs of three men: an anonymous *brāhmaṇa* of the Yajurveda, and Śāṇḍilya and Yājñavalkya of the Śatapatha Brāhmaṇa.

The Final Gnosis

The thoughts of the anonymous *brāhmaṇa* were expressed in Yajurveda XL, which was transferred to the body of Upaniṣadic literature as the Īśa Upaniṣad. It was customary for each *brāhmaṇa* to express, on his death-bed, a final gnosis which was to be the epitome of the truth mastered in a lifetime (or perhaps several lifetimes). Because of a special verse (Y.V. XL,15) we know that the anonymous *brāhmaṇa* was thinking of his death, and we find two authoritative teachers of the Śatapatha Brāhmaṇa following the tradition. Śāṇḍilya's words are in the tenth *kāṇḍa*, and Yājñavalkya's in the final *kāṇḍa*. Yājñavalkya's writings were to be called the Bṛhadāraṇyaka Upaniṣad.[12]

The. words of the anonymous *brāhmaṇa* have been variously translated, nevertheless certain emphases have remained constant. These emphases are:

1. *The name given to divine reality*: Īśa (lord) who envelops all creation. (Y.V. XL,1)
2. *The ideal* is to identify one's self with the self in all creatures. (Y.V. XL, 6)
3. *Death-bed affirmation*: "My breath reach everlasting air." (Y.V. XL,15)
4. *Phrases reminiscent of the ritual*: "By goodly path lead us to riches." (Y.V. XL,16)

5. *Phrases reminiscent of Brahmanic speculation*: "Spirit in yonder sun." (Y.V. XL, 17)
6. *Ideas basic to Upaniṣadic phraseology*: "Motionless yet moving" and "far distant and near." (Y.V. XL,5)

Śāṇḍilya softened the destiny of those who do not know the self by stating that a man receives according to his understanding :

> Let him meditate upon the 'true Brahman.' Now, man here, indeed, is possessed of understanding, and according to how great his understanding is when he departs this world, so does he, on passing away, enter yonder world.
>
> Let him meditate on the Self, which is made up of intelligence, and endowed with a body of spirit, with a form of light, and with an etherial nature, which changes its shape at will, is swift as thought, of true resolve, and true purpose, which consists of all sweet odours and tastes, which holds sway over all regions and pervades this whole universe, which is speechless and indifferent : even as a grain of rice, or a grain of barley, or a grain of millet, or the smallest granule of millet, so is this golden Puruṣa in the heart; even as a smokeless light, it is greater than the sky, greater than the ether, greater than the earth, greater than all existing things : that self of the spirit (breath) is my self: on passing away from hence I shall obtain that self. Verily, whosoever has this trust, for him there is no uncertainty. Thus spake Sāndilya, and so it is.
>
> (X, 6.3.1 and 2)

Arranged (for the purpose of comparison) in an order identical with that of the anonymous brāhmaṇa. (above p. 115) Śāṇḍilya's emphases are these:

1. *The name given to divine reality* : Brahman.
2. *The ideal* is that the personal self and the self of the spirit are identical.
3. *Death-bed affirmation*: If the alternate translation "breath" is read for "spirit," this is verse 15 of Y.V. XL.

4. *Phrases reminiscent of the ritual*: "golden puruṣa."
5. *Phrases reminiscent of Brahmanic speculation*: "breath to air."
6. *Ideas basic to Upaniṣadic phraseology*: "grain of rice;" "greater than all existing things."

In contrast to the gentle Śāṇḍilya we find Yājñavalkya, large as life, quarrelling with his own teacher, contesting in theological disputes, teaching at the court of King Janaka, and finally preparing to enter the forest and devote the remainder of his life to a way of renunciation. We should note that he did not come by the Brahman-Ātman doctrine after he had renounced his active participation in the sacrificial system, but had learned or developed his doctrine *during his active lifetime* of participation in rituals and debate, since he is reputed to have taught his doctrine to his wife, Maitreyī, before entering the forest.[13]

Yājñavalkya finalized the Brahmanic speculation on "sleep."

> The Spirit of man has two dwellings: this world and the world beyond. There is also a third dwelling place: the land of sleep and dreams. Resting in this borderland the Spirit of man can behold his dwelling in this world and in the other world afar, and wandering in this borderland he beholds behind him the sorrows of this world and in front of him he sees the joys of the beyond.[14]

And again:

> While one is in the state of dream, the golden, self-luminous being, the Self within, makes the body to sleep, though he himself remains forever awake and watches by his own light the impressions of deeds that have been left upon the mind. Thereafter, associating himself again with the consciousness of the organs of sense, the Self causes the body to awake.[15]

If the vital airs fail to return power of activity to the senses or the Self fails to associate itself with the consciousness of the organs, does the body fail to wake? In other words, is one then left with the Self as the experiencer as in dreams, or as an alternative, to experience clinical death. Because the thought patterns are so similar, a comparison may be made with the thoughts of a modern biologist, Lyall Watson, who concluded that should a disembodied personality survive after death, our only means of making a biological comparison would be by comparing the experience we know in our dreams.[16]

Is it possible that we have identical suppositions from a *brāhmaṇa* of the ancient world and a modern biologist?

Yājñavalkya's emphases in the areas already shown for the anonymous *brāhmaṇa* (above p. 115) and for Śāṇḍilya (above p. 116) were as follows:

1. *The name given to divine reality*: Brahman is supreme and that Brahman is the Brahman (n) who emanates by means of name and form. This Brahman is the self of all beings. "This universe, before it was created, existed as Brahman. 'I am Brahman' : thus did Brahman know himself. Knowing himself, he became the Self of all beings. Among the gods, he who awakened to the knowledge of the Self became Brahman; and the same was true among the seers."[17]
2. *The ideal*: The individual who recognizes the self is no longer individual. "Where there is consciousness of the Self, individuality is no more."[18] And the identification of all "selves" is complete: "By whom, O my beloved, shall the Knower be known?"[19]
3. *Death-bed affirmation*: The departure of life from the body became a beautiful happening: "Then at the point of the heart a light shines, and this light illumines the soul on its way afar. When departing, by the head, or by the eye or other parts of the body, life arises and follows the soul, and the powers of life follow life. The soul becomes conscious and enters into Consciousness. His wisdom and works take him by the hand, and the knowledge known of old."[20] " . . . . Desiring only the Self, he goes to no other world. Realizing Brahman, he becomes Brahman."[21]

4. *Phrases reminiscent of the ritual*: Yājñavalkya expounded his doctrine with particulars which must have been daily heard and meditated upon in the ritual actions, for he told Maitreyī that, when the drum is beaten the totality of the sound is heard and not the individual beat, and that when the conch shell is blown, the totality, not the notes is heard.[22] He indicated that he accepted the Ṛgveda and the Yajurveda. "As smoke and sparks arise from a lighted fire kindled with damp fuel, even so, Maitreyi, have been breathed forth from the Eternal all knowledge and all wisdom—what we know as the Rigveda, the Yajurveda, and the rest. They are the breath of the Eternal."[23] Even the bird form of the fire altar was used figuratively: "as a hawk or falcon flying in the sky."[24] These are not the phrases a man would choose whose thinking is totally opposed to the ritual system.
5. *Phrases reminiscent of Brahmanic speculation*: Compare Yājñavalkya's description of Brahman (above p. 118, 1) with X, 2.3.9 ff.
6. *Ideas basic to Upaniṣadic phraseology*: Yājñavalkya's teachings are rich in metaphor and uncontrastable contrasts which give a vivid rhythm to the emphasis he is making.

In addition to the Brahmanic speculation of what in man is mortal, what is immortal, Yājñavalkya proposed the self-luminous being:

> The self-luminous being who dwells within the lotus of the heart, surrounded by the senses and sense organs, and who is the light of the intellect, is that Self. Becoming identified with the intellect, he moves to and fro, through birth and death, between this world and the next.[25]

Re-incarnation was affirmed, but with the emphasis on re-birth, not re-death.

> A man acts according to the desires to which he clings. After death he goes to the next world bearing in his mind the

> subtle impressions of his deeds; and after reaping there the harvest of his deeds, he returns again to this world of action. Thus he who has desires continues subject to rebirth.[26]

And, finally, Yājñavalkya stated his doctrine of identification.

> The Self, the great unborn, the undecaying, the undying, the immortal, the fearless, is, in very truth, Brahman. He who knows Brahman is without fear. He who knows Brahman becomes Brahman![27]

A Tentative Summation

Perhaps, over a period of time, the *brāhmaṇas* became aware that the impetus of the sacrificial ritual was diminishing and the Śatapatha Brāhmaṇa possibly came into being as a commentary when knowledge of the meaning of the sacrificial system was faltering and when a new generation, in failing to understand its significance, required an older group to systemise their knowledge. Because of the Brahmanic speculative commentaries, new ideas, beliefs, and philosophies emerged.

When divine reality can be expressed with such diversity and defined in almost any form, or lack of form, it seems futile to consider if any quintessential description of the beliefs of the *brāhmaṇas* is possible. The chameleon-like qualities of the literature and its contradictory nature which fascinate and frustrate those seeking to make coherence of it, would seem to deny the possibility of such a summation. Yet, despite the thousands of words with which the *brāhmaṇas* embroidered their beliefs surrounding their rituals, and with which they obscured their philosophical speculations, a few self-obvious signposts can be demonstrated so simply that one hardly dares to draw attention to them.

For instance, the Śatapatha Brāhmaṇa is literally of "*one hundred* paths, lessons, or ways." In the East, *the* path, *the* road, *the* vehicle, has often symbolized a doctrine's entire content. There was, therefore, a reason why the Śatapatha Brāhmaṇa should become known as "one hundred" that is, "several" or "unlimited." Either it was a friendly appellation, signifying that the *brāhmaṇas* would not limit the ways to divine reality or it was an unfriendly, derogatory title signifying an inability to come to a conclusion about any one method. Whether the title had been intended as positive or negative, the underlying truth is consistent: the Brāhmaṇa affirmed that many paths led to divine reality.

Of these many paths a man (despite ritual restrictions) discovered for himself the *one path* which suited his own requirements. The anonymous *brāhmaṇa* sought a "goodly path" fit for the "man not led astray by sin." (Y.V. XL, 16). The path of the *agnicit* was to be borne on the wings of the bird-altar to the sun and the world beyond. Yājñavalkya found "the small path known of old that stretches far away. By it the sages who know the Spirit rise to the regions of heaven, and thence beyond to liberation."[28] Yājñavalkya's path was not difficult, steep, or thorny (as might be expected because of the ascetic tradition in both Hinduism and Buddhism) but it was "adorned with white and blue, yellow and green and red."[29]

Follow the man who follows the rainbow!

We have also observed the importance given to the correct state of mind with which to meet death and to the seer's death-bed avowal, in which he traditionally affirmed his doctrine and concentrated upon this core of affirmation as the spirit departed from his body. Recall again Śāṇḍilya's words: "At the moment of death a knower of Brahman should meditate upon the true Brahman... that self of the spirit is my self... on passing away from hence I shall obtain that self." (X, 6.3.1-2)

The limits of meaning which could be affixed to words derived from the root $\sqrt{}$*bṛh* had not been fixed. The *brāhmaṇas* created a new, or re-generated an old neuter form of $\sqrt{}$*bṛh*, endowing it with a cosmological concept of divine reality—eternal, infinite, total, transcendent, and immanent—so that, whatever may happen to the *brāhmaṇa* (caste) or Brahmin (priest) a word from the same root would hold supreme position in a new era. By that one word alone they gained immortality. The word is Brahman.

CHAPTER VII

References and Notes

1. F. J. Streng, "The Problem of Symbolic Structures in Religious Apprehension," *History of Religions* (Vol. IV, No. 1, 1964-65) p. 126.

2. "Theistic" used in this sense : "Theism : Belief in existence of a god supernaturally revealed to man and sustaining a personal relation to his creatures." *Concise Oxford Dictionary* : (5th ed. 1964).

3. Indian religion has traditionally considered man ignorant rather than sinful, however, there are many mentions of "sin" in the Śatapatha Brāhmaṇa. For example, II, 5.2.20 where a woman who commits adultery sins against Varuṇa, and XIII, 3.1.1 where the sin of killing a Brahmin or *brāhmaṇa* is expiated by the Aśvamedha.

4. The Pūrva Mīmāṁsā, the Philosophical School based on a return to the ritual, would seem to conflict with this statement since the school is reportedly atheistic or agnostic. However, the existence of deities was not denied : "Deities cannot sacrifice, because apart from themselves, there are no other Deities to whom they could offer Sacrifice—and there can be no offering to one's own self." Sir Ganganatha Jha, *Pūrva-mīmāṁsā in its Sources*, Vol. I, p. 307. For the theological viewpoint of sacrificing to oneself, compare Odin, Puruṣa, and Prajāpati.

5. Ibid, p. 306. Compare the answer given to the question "What is heaven?" "The established conclusion on this point is that the term 'heaven' stands only for a form of happiness."

6. "As to this they say, 'One death, or many?'" (X, 5.2.16)

7. As late as XII, 8.1.19 the Fathers continue to live with Yama. From the Ṛgvedic age, life with Yama appears to be thought of as in bodily form. My point is that new speculation is questioning such beliefs.

8. *Larousse Encyclopedia of Mythology*, p. 31.

9. Eggeling, Part V, p. 339, fn. 3.

10. Dowson : *A Classical Dictionary of Hindu Mythology* : Brahma(n).

11. I have avoided the use of the word "pantheism" because of what I believe to be unfortunate uses of the word, e.g., Macdonell, *A Vedic Reader*, p. 195, where the commentary on the Puruṣa Sūkta, X.90, concludes with these words : "The religious view is moreover different from that of the old hymns for it is pantheistic; 'Puruṣa is all this world, what has been and what shall be.' It is, in fact, the starting point of the pantheistic philosophy of India." I think this ignores the fact that only part of Puruṣa is the basis for creation, that is, while all creation is god, god should be recognized as being more than the total of creation. In *The Vedic Rishi*, I have discussed religious and mystical states in relation to the experience of the devotee.

12. "The remaining six chapters of the last book of the (Śatapatha) Brāhmaṇa form the so-called Bṛhad-āraṇyaka." Eggeling, Part V, Intro i.

How close is the relationship of the Bṛhadāraṇyaka Upaniṣad and the Śatapatha Brāhmaṇa can be inferred from this comment on the Vedic accent : "The accent is marked in all the texts of the four Vedas as well as in two Brāhmaṇas, the Taittirīya (including its Āraṇyaka) and the Śatapatha (including the Bṛhadāraṇyaka Upaniṣad)." A. A. Macdonell, *A Vedic Grammar for Students*, p. 448.

13. Bṛhadāraṇyaka Upaniṣad, cited by Swami Prabhavananda and F. Manchester, translators, *The Upaniṣads, Breath of the Eternal*, p. 86.
14. Juan Mascaro, *The Upaniṣads*, p. 134.
15. Prabhavananda and Manchester, *The Upaniṣads*, p. 105.
16. Lyall Watson, *The Romeo Error*, p. 105.
17. Prabhavananda and Manchester, *The Upaniṣads*, pp. 80-81.
18. Ibid, p. 88.
19. Ibid, p. 89.
20. Mascaro, *The Upaniṣads*, p. 139.
21. Prabhavananda and Manchester, *The Upaniṣads*, p. 109.
22. Ibid, p. 88.
23. Ibid, p. 88.
24. Ibid, p. 107.
25. Ibid, p. 104.
26. Ibid, p. 109.
27. Ibid, pp. 111, 112.
28. Mascaro, *The Upaniṣads*, p. 140.
29. Ibid, p. 140.

BIBLIOGRAPHY

Aggarwal, H. R. *A Short History of Sanskrit Literature*. Delhi: Munshi Ram Manohar Lal, 1939.

Arguelles, J. and M. *Mandala*. Berkeley and London: Shambala, 1972.

Arnold, Sir Edwin. *The Light of Asia*. London: Routledge & Kegan Paul, 1971.

Bhattacharji, S. *The Indian Theogony*. Cambridge University Press, 1970.

Bose, A. C. *Hymns from the Vedas*. Bombay: Asia Publishing House, 1966.

Brandon, S. G. F. *Creation Legends of the Ancient Near East*. Wilde Lectures in Natural and Comparative Religion, Oxford. Manchester University Press, 1962.
"Sacrifice." *A Dictionary of Comparative Religion* edited by S. G. F. Brandon. London: Weidenfeld & Nicolson, 1970.

Brown, W. Norman. "Mythology of India," *Mythologies of the Ancient World*, edited and introduced by S. N. Kramer. New York: Doubleday & C., 1961.

Caland, W. "Corrections of Eggeling's Translation of the Śatapathabrāhmaṇa," *Bulletin of The School of Oriental Studies, London Institution*. London: Kraus Reprint Ltd., 1964. VI (1930-32) p. 297.

Cammann, S. "Islamic and Indian Magic Squares, Parts I and II." *History of Religions, An International Journal for Comparative Historical Studies*, edited by M. Eliade, J. Kitagawa, C. Long, University of Chicago Press. VIII (1969-1970) No. 2, p. 181 and No. 4, p. 271.

Campbell, Joseph. *The Masks of God, Vol II: Oriental Mythology*. London: Secker & Warburg, 1962.

Caster, J. *Wings of the Falcon*. New York: Holt, 1968.

Chaitanya, K. *A New History of Sanskrit Literature*. Bombay: Asia Publishing House, 1962.

Church, Canon Ivor. "The Problems Arising from the Use of Symbols in the Church". An address delivered to the Faith and Order Commision, 1974.

Cirlot, J. E. *A Dictionary of Symbols*, translated by Jack Sage. New York: Philosophical Library, 1962.

Compton. G. B. "The Cult of Sun Worship in the Rigveda." Unpublished Honours Thesis, University of Queensland, 1977.

Converse, H. C. "The Agnicayana Rite; Indigenous Origins?" *History of Religions, An International Journal for Comparative Historical Studies*, edited by M. Eliade, J. Kitagawa, C. Long, University of Chicago Press. XIV (1974-75) No. 2, p. 81.

Coomaraswamy, A. K. *A New Approach to the Vedas*. London: Luzac & Co., 1933.

Danielou, A. *Hindu Polytheism*. Bollingen Series LXXII. Princeton University Press, 1964.

von Daniken, E. *Chariots of the Gods?* London: Corgi, 1972.

Davidson, H. R. Ellis. *Gods and Myths of Northern Europe*. London: Penguin, 1964.

Davies, C. C. *The Historical Atlas of the Indian Peninsula*. Oxford University Press, 1949.

Dowson, J. *A Classical Dictionary of Hindu Mythology*. 11th edn. London: Routledge & Kegan Paul, 1968.

Drury, Naama Mrs. Joan Kenny. *The Vedic Rishi*. Wellington Point: Orchid Enterprises, 1974.

Durkheim, Emile. *The Elementary Forms of the Religious Life*, translated by J. W. Swain. New York: Collier Books, 1961.

Dutt, R.C. *A History of Civilisation in Ancient India*. 2 vols. 1st Indian reprint. Delhi: Vishal Publishers, 1972.

Dutt, R. *Mahabharata, the Epic of India*. London : Dent, 1899.

Eliade, Mircea. *Cosmos and History : The Myth of the Eternal Return*. New York: Harper and Row Torchbacks, 1959.
Shamanism—Archaic Techniques of Ecstasy. translated by W. R. Trash. London : Routledge & Kegan Paul, 1964.

Yoga, Immortality and Freedom. Princeton University Press, 1969.

From Primitive to Zen. New York: Harper & Row, 1967.

Elkin, A. P. *The Australian Aborigine.* reprint. 4th edn. Sydney: Angus & Robertson, 1966.

Embree, A. T. *The Hindu Tradition.* New York : The Modern Library, 1966.

The Encyclopedia of Religion edited by Vergilius Ferm. New Jersey: Adams & Co, 1959.

The Encyclopedia of Religion and Ethics, XII vols. edited by J. Hastings. Edinburgh: Clark, 1957.

Farquhar, J. N. *Outline of the Religious Literature of India.* Oxford University Press. 1920.

The Crown of Hinduism. Delhi: Motilal Banarsidass, 1967.

Finegan, J. *The Archeology of World Religions,* Vols. I-III. Princeton University Press, 1952.

Frazer, Sir James George. *The Golden Bough, a Study in Magic and Religion.* 2nd edn. London: Macmillan, 1907.

Freud, Sigmund. *Totem and Taboo.* translated by J. Strachey. New York: Norton & Company Inc., 1950.

Fulcher, R. W. "The Contribution of Rene Guenon." Lecture, History of Religions, University of Queensland, 1974.

Ghose, N. *The Aryan Trail in Iran and India.* University of Calcutta, 1937.

Goldstucker, T. *Inspired Writings of Hinduism.* Calcutta: Susil Gupta, 1958.

Gonda, J. *Epithets in the Rigveda.* The Hague: Mouton & Co., 1959.

Change and Continuity in Indian Religion. The Hague: Mouton & Co., 1965.

Grierson, G. A "The Monotheistic Religion of Ancient India and Its Descendant the Modern Hindu Doctrine of Faith." Paper presented at the 3rd International Conference of History of Religions. Oxford, 1908. London : British Museum.

Griffith, R. T. H. Translator. *The Texts of the White Yajurveda*. 3rd edn. Benares: E. J. Lazarus & Co., 1957.

Guerber, A. A. *The Myths of Greece and Rome*. London: Harrap, 1907.

Guthrie, W. K. G. *The Greeks and Their Gods*. London: Methuen & Co., Ltd., University Paperback edn., 1968.

von Hagen, Victor Wolfgang. *The Ancient Sun Kingdoms of the Americas*. London: Panther, 1967.

Halpin, T. A. Technical Secretary, Astronomers' Association of Queensland. Letter dated 19.2.74.

Hopkins, E. W. *Epic Mythology*. New York: Biblo & Tanner, 1969.

Hubert, H. and Mauss, M. *Sacrifice, Its Nature and Function*, translated by W. D. Halls. London: Cohen & West, 1964.

Jacobi, J. *Complex, Archetypes, and Symbols in the Psychology of C. G. Jung*. London: Routledge & Kegan Paul, 1967.

James, E. O. *The Nature and Function of Priesthood*. London: Thames and Hudson, 1956.

Myth and Ritual in the Ancient Near East. London: Thames and Hudson, 1958.

The Cult of the Mother Goddess. London: Thames and Hudson, 1959.

Sacrifice and Sacrament. Thames and Hudson, 1962.

Origins of the Sacrifice. London: Thames and Hudson, 1971.

James, W. *The Varieties of Religious Experience*. London: Longmans & Green, 1902.

Jha, Sir Ganganatha. *Pūrva-mīmāṁsā in its Sources*. Vol. I of *Library of Indian Philosophy and Religion* edited by S. Radhakrishnan, Delhi, 1942.

Jung, C. G. *The Archetypes and the Collective Unconscious* Vol. IX of *The Collected Works of C. G. Jung*. Bollingen Series 20. New York: Pantheon, 1958.

Psychology and Religion West and East Vol. XI of *The Collected Works of C. G. Jung*. Bollingen Series 20. New York: Pantheon, 1958.

Man and His Symbols edited by C. G. Jung. London: Aldus Books Ltd., 1964.

Memories, Dreams, and Reflections, recorded and edited by A. Jaffe. London: Fontana Library, 1967.

The Kama Sutra of Vatsyayana, introduced by F. S. Klaf. New York: Lancer Books, 1968.

Kane, P. V. *The History of the Dharmaśāstra*, Vol. II, Parts 1 and 2. Poona : Bhandarkar Oriental Research Institute, 1941.

Kardiner, Abram and Preble, Edward. *They Studied Man.* New York: Mentor Books, 1963.

Keith, A. B. *The Religion and Philosophy of the Veda and Upanisads.* 2 vols. Harvard Oriental Series, 1925.

de Kleen, T. *Mudras.* New York: University Books, 1970.

Klepesta J. and Rukl, A. *Constellations.* London: Paul Hamlyn, 1972.

Kristensen, W. Brede. *The Meaning of Religion.* Reprint. The Hague: Martinus Nijhoff, 1971.

Lanman, C. B. "Beginnings of Hindu Pantheism." A Paper presented to the 22nd Annual Meeting of the American Philological Association, 1890. Archives: British Museum.

Lommel, A. *Prehistoric and Primitive Man.* London: Paul Hamlyn, 1966.

Lynch, J. Editor. *The Coffee Table Book of Astrology.* London: Weidenfeld & Nicolson, 1962.

Macdonald, K. S. *Sacred Books of the East, Examined and Described.* London and Madras: The Christian Literature Society for India, 1896.

Macdonell, A. A. *A Vedic Reader for Students.* 7th imp. London: Oxford University Press, 1970.

A Vedic Grammar. Oxford University Press, 1966.

A Practical Sanskrit Dictionary. Oxford University Press, 1971.

Mackenzie, D. A. *India, Myths and Legends.* London: Graham, 1913.

Macnicol, N. *Hindu Scriptures.* London: Everyman's Library, 1969.

Mainkar, R. G. *Mysticism in the Rigveda.* Bombay : Popular Book Depot, 1961.

Marshall, Sir John. *Mohenjo-daro and the Indus Civilization.* 3 Vols. London: Prolesthain, 1931.

Mascaro, Juan. *The Upaniṣads.* Middlesex: Penguin Classics, 1934.

Maurice, David [U Ohn Ghine]. *The Lion's Roar.* London: Rider, 1962.

Michener, J. A. *The Source.* London: Corgi (Reprint), 1974.

Miller, M. J. *The Southern Sky.* Melbourne: Heinemann, 1972.

Moore, P. *The Southern Stars.* South Australia: Rigby, 1972.

Neumann, Erich. *The Great Mother.* Translated by R. Manheim. London: Routledge & Kegan Paul, 1964.

New Larousse Encyclopedia of Mythology. Introduced by Robert Graves. London: Paul Hamlyn, 1968.

Nietzsche. *Thus Spoke Zarathustra.* Translated by R. J. Hollingdale. Middlesex: Penguin, 1961.

O'Brien, E. *Varieties of Mystic Experience.* New York: Mentor Omega, 1965.

Otto, Rudolf. *Mysticism, East and West.* Oxford University Press, 1932.

The Idea of the Holy. Translated by J. W. Harvey. Oxford University Press, 1972.

Pauwels, L. and Bergier, J. *The Morning of the Magicians.* London: Granada, 1971.

Perry, E. L. *A Sanskrit Primer.* Columbia University Press, 1965.

Piggot, S. *Prehistoric India.* London: Cassell, 1962.

Prabhavananda, Swami and Manchester, F. *The Upaniṣads, Breath of the Eternal.* 8th printing. New York: New American Library, 1957.

Phillips, David, "Scapegoat," *Man, Myth & Magic*, ed. R. Cavendish. London: Purnell, 1970.

Radhakrishnan, S. *Eastern Religion and Western Thought.* Oxford University Press, 1939.

The Hindu View of Life. London: Unwin, 1971.

Rakoczi, B. I. "Divination." *Man, Myth and Magic*, edited by Richard Cavendish. London: Purnell, 1970.

Renou. L. *Vedic India*, translated by P. Spratt. Calcutta: Susil Gupta, 1957.

Robinson, T. H. *A Short Comparative History of Religions*. 2nd edn. London: Duckworth, 1951.

Sarkar, S. "Antiquity of Hindu Civilization—An Astronomical Assessment." *Journal of the Bharat Sevashram Sangha*, edited by Swami Purnananda. May-June, 1974. London. The Bharat Sevashram Sangha.

Sastri, G. *A Concise History of Sanskrit Literature*. Oxford University Press, 1960.

Shankara. *Crest Jewel of Discrimination*, translated by Swami Prabhavananda and C. Isherwood. New York : Mentor, 1947.

Sharpe, E. J. "Sacrifice." *Man, Myth and Magic*, edited by Richard Cavendish. London: Purnell, 1970.

Skolnick, B. Brisbane Hebrew Congregation. Letter dated 16-11-73.

Spencer, S. *Mysticism in World Religions*. Middlesex: Pelican, 1963.

Streng, F. J. "The Problems of Symbolic Structures in Religious Apprehension." *History of Religions, An International Journal for Comparative Historical Studies*, edited by M. Eliade, J. Kitagawa, C. Long, University of Chicago Press. IV (1964-65) No. 2, p. 126.

Sullivan, H. P. "A Re-examination of the Religion of the Indus Civilization." *History of Religions, An International Journal for Comparative Historical Studies*, edited by M. Eliade, J. Kitagawa, C. Long, University of Chicago Press. IV (1964-65) No. 1, p. 18.

Thomas, P. *Indian Women Through the Ages*. Bombay : Asia Publishing House, 1971.

de Vaux, R. *Studies in Old Testament Sacrifice*. University of Wales Press, 1964.

Walker, B. *Hindu World—An Encyclopedic Survey of Hinduism*. 2 Vols. London: Allen and Unwin, 1968.

Watson, L. *Supernature*. London: Coronet, 1974.

The Romeo Error. London; Coronet III imp., 1976.

Weber, A. *The History of Indian Literature*, translated by J. Mann and T. Zachariae, Chowkhamba Sanskrit Series. India: 1878.

Woolley, Sir Charles. *Ur of the Chaldees*. London: Ernest Benn Ltd., 1929.

Yerkes, R. K. *Sacrifice in Greek and Roman Religions and Early Judaism*. London: Luzac & Co., 1938.

Zaehner, R. C. *Mysticism, Sacred and Profane*. Oxford University Press, 1961.

Hinduism. Oxford University Press, 1962.

Hindu Scriptures. London: Dent. 1966.

Zimmer, Heinrich. *Myths and Symbols in Indian Art and Civilisation*, edited by Joseph Campbell. Bollingen Series VI, Princeton University Press, 1972.

Philosophies of India, edited by Joseph Campbell, Bollingen Series XXVI. Princeton University Press, 1975.

INDEX

INDEX